complete
Mike Davis and Guy Andrews
MOUNTAIN BIKE
maintenance

Note

Whilst every effort has been made to ensure that the content of this book is as technically accurate and as sound as possible, neither the author nor the publishers can accept responsibility for any injury or loss sustained as a result of the use of this material.

Published by Bloomsbury Publishing Plc

50 Bedford Square
London WC1B 3DP
www.bloomsbury.com

First edition 2013

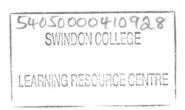

ISBN (print): 978 1 4081 7097 7
ISBN (epub): 978 1 4081 8645 9
ISBN (epdf): 978 1 4081 8644 2

A CIP catalogue record for this book is available from the British Library.

Cover photographs © Gerard Brown, Genesis Bikes and Shutterstock
Inside photographs © Gerard Brown with the exception of
p9, 13: Trek Bicycle Corporation (www.trekbikes.com)
p10, top: Cannondale (www.cannondale.com)
p10, bottom: Santa Cruz Bicycles (www.santacruzbikes.com)
p11 Genesis Bikes (www.genesisbikes.co.uk)
p12, top; p14 bottom: Kona (www.konaworld.com)
p12, bottom: Ridgeback (www.ridgeback.co.uk)
p14, top: Islabikes (www.islabikes.co.uk)

Designed by Jonathan Briggs

This book is produced using paper that is made from wood grown in managed, sustainable forests. It is natural, renewable and recyclable. The logging and manufacturing processes conform to the environmental regulations of the country of origin.

Typeset in 12pt on 9.5pt Helvetica Neue LT Pro by Jonathan Briggs, London
Printed in China by South China Printing Company, Dongguan Guangdong
10 9 8 7 6 5 4 3 2 1

FOREWORD

Mountain biking: Why do we do it?

We are away from the cops, the cars and the concrete.
We dip into the endorphin pool.
We have uninterrupted time with our buds.
We get way out in the woods, ripping and tearing, air time,
riding the natural rollercoaster to quiet places we have never been.

This is how it is and how it's always been. It's about self-sufficiency,
your own power and your machine. Learn more about them and you
are a free bird.

In the old days you would start a ride with six riders and three would finish
walking with broken parts in their hands. The bikes weighed around 50lb
– we called them Klunkers. The gears ground, grated and hated you, the
brakes squealed and you had to stop on the downhills and wave your
hands around to stop the numbness. Parts that were never intended for
this use/abuse would crack and come flying apart. We were in the middle
of nowhere – ride Pine Mountain and you might see a hiker or maybe no-
one all day. When one of us broke down our attitude was 'We have all day
to fix it' or 'Do you want to walk out?' The creative repair ruled: Stuffing
grass into a flat tyre after the last inner tube was used, or using the baling
wire from a California rural fence, or forming a fix with Manzenita tree limbs
with the use of the Klunker multi-tool, a pair of vise grips.

That was 30 years ago. Since then, the Klunker has transformed into
the Mountain Bike and thousands of creative minds have pored over
every detail. The new bikes almost float up the climbs, the feeling of
flying comes often, full suspension really works for the rider and at the
end of the day you will be riding your bike better on 99 out of 100 rides
if you know what you are doing.

That's what this book is all about: What to look for on a day-to-day
basis, the preparation and upkeep that keeps the ride sweet. Guy
Andrews cuts to the chase, with his real-world experience and intimate
knowledge of the bits and pieces and how and where they play. Guy
advises how and when to fix it and when it's advisable to seek help and
go to your local wrench.

The knowledge in this book is the stuff that makes today's bikes work
like they should. It is the stuff you wish came in the owner's manual
instead of the legalese that a maker is obliged to include. Every
mountain bike needs this book, for it will be happier and so will you.

Gary Fisher

Preface to the second edition

Since the original edition of this book was published, a great deal has changed in the world of mountain biking. Disc brakes were popular then but all but ubiquitous now. 29in wheels have gone from an uncertain niche to mainstream dominance, and there's a third wheel size – 650B – gaining traction. Multiple new headset and bottom bracket standards have emerged as manufacturers attempt to outdo each other's stiffness-to-weight ratios. Remotely-adjustable seatposts, new shock technology, through-axle wheels for trails bikes... The list goes on. It's no surprise, then, that this second edition of *Complete Mountain Bike Maintenance* is fatter than the first – we've taken very little out but put a lot of new material in. Some chapters were in danger of getting rather unwieldy, so we've reorganised what goes where and shuffled the more common jobs towards the beginnings of chapters with a view to making things easier to find.

Every mountain biker should be able to work on their own bike, even if it's just the simple things.
We hope this book will give you the confidence to have a go.

Mike Davis and Guy Andrews

Acknowledgements

Sincerest thanks to all the companies who supplied bikes and equipment to help in the making of this book: Madison (Shimano, Park Tools, Genesis and Ridgeback bikes and a whole pile of other stuff); Trek (bikes and shoes); ATB Sales (Marin and Whyte bikes); DMR (bikes and components); Fisher Outdoor Leisure (SRAM); Cambrian (Continental tyres); Silverfish (Race Face, Rock'n'Roll lubes); Chicken & Sons (Mavic, Time, Sapim); Cycling Sports Group (Cannondale).

Special thanks to photographer Gerard Brown – without his patience, experience and attention to detail this book wouldn't have been as well illustrated – and Jonathan Briggs for tireless layout work (and frequent rejigging thereof).

Guy would like to thank Frank Hornby, the inventor of Meccano, for inspiring him in things mechanical, and his dad, Keith Andrews, who taught him the benefits of both reading and ignoring instruction manuals.

Mike would also like to thank his dad, Bob Davis, from whom he appears to have got a desire for taking things apart (and sometimes putting them back together again). Also Sandra for her deep reserves of patience and encouragement, and Isla and Oscar for reminding him about the simple fun of riding bikes.

CONTENTS

THE MOUNTAIN BIKE

The mountain bike was one of those ideas that was bound to happen eventually. Riding bicycles off road is a very old idea – they came along before Tarmac roads, after all, and cyclocross racing has seen bikes competing in the mud for nearly a century. Over the years, various people have cobbled motorbike handlebars onto old road bikes to create 'trackers' for hacking round the woods, but it took a bunch of Californian cyclists looking for new bike-related entertainment in the 1970s to take the first step on the path to the modern mountain bike.

They hit upon the notion of dragging pre-war beach cruisers up the mountains of Marin County in order to race them back down the steep, loose fire roads. With just the one gear, getting to the start line involved either a pickup truck or pushing. The backpedal coaster brakes that were fine when pootling along on the flat proved incapable of sustained mountain descending, tending to overheat. The requirement to repack the hubs with grease gave the most famous early race – the Repack – its name.

Technology moved quickly in the early days. Grafting on cantilever brakes from touring bikes and pulling them with motorbike levers improved control immeasurably, especially when a source of aluminium rims was found. The big leap, though, was fitting derailleur gears, allowing the bikes to be pedalled up the mountains as well as down them. Those early 'clunkers' may have been cobbled together, but it wasn't long before purpose-built bikes appeared from local framebuilders. Within a few years, mountain bikes were being mass-produced overseas and the boom was on.

The pace of development has remained high ever since. Modern bikes feature up to 30 gears, hydraulic disc brakes and suspension at both wheels. Aluminium has taken over from steel as the dominant frame material, with carbon fibre common on high-end bikes. Mountain bikes are lighter and stronger then ever before.

But mountain bikes do go wrong. No matter how tough they are, eventually the components may fail, wear out or break. This easy-to-follow, step-by-step guide to fixing your mountain bike will help to keep you riding. We'll take you from the basic checkups through to advanced repairs and trailside fixes. However, prevention is always better than cure, so we'll also show you how to keep your bike clean, well adjusted and free from trouble.

TYPES OF MOUNTAIN BIKE

In the early days of mountain biking, there was just one kind of mountain bike. As the sport has diversified, various sub-genres and niches have formed, each with their particular strengths and weaknesses. If you're starting out, a trail or cross-country bike is the best choice – they're the most versatile.

FULL-SUSPENSION TRAIL BIKE

The full-suspension trail bike is the closest thing to the original go anywhere, do anything mountain bike. Despite having 120-140mm of suspension travel at each end, trail bikes are still light enough to tackle long climbs easily – except budget models, most are under 13kg (29lb) and more expensive bikes with carbon fibre frames can be well below that.

The suspension fork and rear shock are often highly adjustable, with different settings for climbing and descending – typically firmer for climbing and softer for descending. Some trail bikes have adjustable travel too, letting you optimise the bike for the terrain.

Trail bikes typically have slightly relaxed steering geometry, giving confidence on descents.

That makes them very at home at purpose-built trail centres, which tend to emphasise descending. Combined with control and comfort from the suspension and the reasonable weight, trail bikes are a great choice for long off-road rides too.

If you're not sure exactly what kind of trails you'll be riding, the all-round trail bike is the best option – it'll tackle pretty much anything, and while other kinds of bikes may be slightly faster over particular kinds of terrain, the trail bike is the most versatile.

ALL-MOUNTAIN BIKE

If your riding is downhill-focused but you need to get to the top under your own steam, an all-mountain bike may be for you. While looking very similar to trail bikes, AM bikes typically have more travel (140-160mm is typical), more robust wheels, larger tyres and more powerful brakes.

The steering geometry of an all-mountain bike is more downhill-oriented than that of a trail bike, with a shallower head angle and shorter stem, but not so much that it struggles on flat trails or climbs. An AM bike will be heavier, though.

It's a good choice for enduro racing, involving timed downhill sections linked by untimed climbs.

DOWNHILL BIKE

Downhill bikes are pure race machines, designed solely to descend as fast as possible. To that end, they have long travel (around 180mm) and a very shallow head angle for stability at speed. Frames have to be extremely strong to handle the loads from twin-crown forks, so inevitably DH bikes are typically heavier than others. They're not as heavy as you might think, though, with professional-level bikes often approaching 16kg (35lb) – pedalling can still make the difference between winning and losing, so racers don't want to carry excess weight. Freeride bikes are similar in terms of travel but have a more robust build to handle huge drops and jumps.

TRAIL HARDTAIL

While full suspension has developed to the point where it has huge performance advantages and few drawbacks, doing without still saves weight and reduces maintenance and cost. The hardtail mountain bike – with a suspension fork but no suspension for the rear wheel – sacrifices a little bit of speed and comfort for the sake of simplicity. For many riders that's a more than worthwhile trade-off. Indeed, lots of hardtail fans express a preference for the ride of an unsuspended bike – you can't rely on the suspension to do all the work, and having to work the bike through rough sections can be very rewarding.

You'll find 100-120mm travel suspension forks (or 80-100mm travel on hardtails with bigger 29in wheels) and similar geometry to full-suspension trail bikes. Trail hardtails are fun bikes to ride, especially on shorter routes. For rides of more than a couple of hours, you'll feel the benefit of full suspension, although that's not to say that hardtails are limiting – you can certainly do big, rough rides on them, it's just that you'll feel the aftermath more keenly the following day.

That aside, trail hardtails are just as effective an all-rounder as their fully-suspended brethren.

DJ/4X

Although looking superficially similar to a conventional hardtail MTB, dirt jump bikes are every bit as specialist as downhill race bikes. They're designed solely for jumping, with steeper geometry for manoeuvrability and a low-slung frame. Some jump bikes are fully rigid, while others include a suspension fork that's usually stiffly sprung to save bad landings. Entry-level models usually have a single chainring and multiple gears at the back, while real dirt jump purists make do with just one gear. Bikes for 4X racing are similar to jump bikes but usually with a lighter build for better acceleration.

URBAN COMMUTER

While not technically a mountain bike, many of the bikes sold for riding on city streets are closely related and share many of the same components. Some of them are essentially mountain bikes fitted with narrower, smooth-treaded tyres for road use, although higher gears are a typical feature too.

While some commuter bikes have suspension forks, they're less useful on road – rigid forks are lighter and require less maintenance. Disc brakes are a common feature on more expensive models, giving strong, consistent braking in all weather conditions. You'll also often find rack and mudguard mounts, which have become something of a rarity on mountain bikes.

XC RACE

For a long time, cross-country (XC) racing was the mainstay of mountain biking, with the ethos of covering mixed terrain as quickly as possible informing the design of bikes for everyone, racers or not. Gradually, though, XC race bikes have become very specialist tools. With cross-country races mostly won on the climbs, XC bikes are almost the exact opposite of DH bikes. Low weight is everything, and steep geometry with low handlebars optimises uphill performance but can be a handful on descents.

Professional racers will choose between hardtails (with 80-100mm forks) or full suspension bikes (80-100mm of travel at both ends) according to the nature of the course – if it's smooth the lighter hardtail is likely to be faster, but rougher courses benefit from full suspension. Full suspension bikes are also a good choice for the longer variations on XC racing, like marathons and 24-hour endurance events.

Big 29in wheels are popular for XC too, with the benefits of easy rolling over bumps outweighing the weight penalty for many riders. While pure XC race bikes are extremely single-minded, most can also make entirely capable all-rounders too. Often a change of handlebar and stem for a more upright riding position and some more robust tyres are all that's needed.

KIDS

The majority of children's bikes are at least styled along mountain bike lines. You wouldn't call most of them mountain bikes, although some high-end models for teenagers are essentially proper MTBs with smaller wheels for a good fit.

While suspension forks are common on kids' bikes, they're usually something of a hindrance, adding weight for little appreciable benefit – it's worth seeking out a model with a rigid fork. We include children's bikes here because they share many components with adult mountain bikes – brakes and gear shifters, for example.

CYCLOCROSS BIKE

Also not a mountain bike is the cyclocross bike, but again there's some parts commonality – brakes (including, increasingly, discs) in particular – so it's worth a mention.

Cyclocross is a sport with a long history, involving short off-road circuits on bikes that look similar to road bikes but have shallower angles and room for bigger, knobbly tyres. Cyclocross racing is quite a niche sport, but the bikes themselves are great all-rounders – they're much faster than mountain bikes on the road and still surprisingly capable off it, even without huge tyres or suspension.

BUYING A BIKE

Supermarkets and car accessory shops are packed with sub-£100 'mountain bikes', but we know from experience that these are best avoided. Typically it takes a good mechanic about an hour to take a good-quality mountain bike from boxed to ready to ride. The same mechanic could easily spend three times that on a £79 bike and still not have something that was capable of being ridden off-road except extremely tentatively – it's just not possible to sell a truly dirt-capable bike that cheaply.

It's also worth remembering that supermarkets don't tend to have experienced mechanics to assemble bikes. You take it home in a box and you're left to your own devices, generally with inadequate instructions. Even if you know what you're doing, the end result will be at best disappointing. If you don't know what you're doing, it's likely to be unsafe.

A 'true' mountain bike will come with full instructions for the consumer, details of any special parts (Shimano usually supplies instructions, and suspension forks normally have their own special instructions too), a PDI (Pre-Delivery Inspection) check list and, lastly, a warranty card. Any bike that can't supply this information should be avoided.

Mountain biking is very hard on your bike and, when your life can depend on the quality and function of the equipment, you need to know you have done everything possible to prevent failure. So, it's far better to use a bike that is up to the job in the first place. This also means a bike that has been professionally assembled and checked from new, which is why your first port of call should be a good local bike shop.

Historically speaking, the entry-level mountain bike has always cost around £350–500. Because this is a very competitive price point these bikes are often very good value, featuring quality parts and a well-made frame. However, entry-level bikes are not designed and built to be pushed to the limits, so as your riding improves you will probably want to upgrade what you ride.

A particular weakness of sub-£500 bikes is the suspension fork. Nearly every entry-level bike has a suspension fork because they look good on the shop floor, but they're usually very heavy, excessively flexible and with a poorly controlled action. Typically they contain steel coil springs and at best a very simple damper, often no damper at all. This makes them so bouncy that they're worse than no suspension at all. Alas, entry-level bikes with rigid forks are thin on the ground.

Remember that your main priorities are the frame, then the suspension forks, then the wheels, then the contact points (saddle, handlebars and pedals) and, lastly, the brakes and transmission components. Components are last on the list because they will wear out in time and, should you want to upgrade them, you can do it when they wear out. The frame, suspension forks and wheels are always the most expensive parts of a bike, so look for the manufacturers that put the most effort into these areas and don't be fooled just because the bike has an XT rear derailleur or the added attraction of (poor-quality) disc brakes.

Look for the details, as sometimes corners are cut to save money – usually where you can't see it or may not notice it, for example the chain or the bottom bracket. Anonymous, unbranded hubs are another common money-saving choice. This isn't such a big deal for front hubs, but the freehub mechanism in the rear hub is often a weak point and spares for no-name hubs can be hard to come by.

WOMEN'S FIT

For many years women had to make do with bikes designed primarily for men, relying on juggling with seatposts and stems to improve the fit.

The average woman is significantly shorter than the average man, and women need a shorter reach to the bars for a given height too. Today most manufacturers have a big choice of women-specific bikes with geometry and sizing adjusted to suit. Don't automatically assume that a women's bike is the right choice just because you're a woman, though – different brands take different approaches to frame geometry, and many women (especially taller ones) find that a man's bike from a particular manufacturer offers the best fit.

Most current Shimano and SRAM mountain bike components are designed specifically for riding off-road. Those two manufacturers dominate the market. Always beware of gear components that you haven't heard of, as they may well just not be a match in quality for the job. Most manufacturers mix and match components from different brands – SRAM chains on Shimano cassettes are common, and chainsets often come from other companies – which is usually fine, although you'll generally get the best performance and reliability by sticking to one brand throughout.

DIRECT SALES OR MAIL ORDER

Some manufacturers sell directly to the public without going via a bike shop at all. Typically this means cheaper bikes for an equivalent specification, but the trade-off is losing the shop's experience and advice. Test rides are also tricky to arrange. You really need to know what you're doing to get the best out of direct sales. Some assembly of the bike is usually required (although it's often minimal, and clear instructions and tools are usually included), and any warranty issues will mean re-boxing the bike and arranging for it to be collected.

Many shops also sell bikes from mainstream brands via mail order, although some brands aren't keen on their bikes being sold this way. The shop should still carry out assembly and pre-delivery inspection before repackaging the bike for delivery, although it's not unheard of for

bikes to arrive on a customer's doorstep in the same state they left the factory in – some way from ready to ride.

SECOND-HAND BIKES

The growth of the internet auction site ebay and classified ads on MTB websites has meant a boom in the used bike market. There's potential to score a real bargain, but if you don't know exactly what you're looking at there are many possible pitfalls. Bikes are often badly (or even deliberately erroneously) described as to their condition or even manufacturer, and if a bike's a long way away you may only have photos from which to gauge the condition.

It's a good idea to stick to bikes local to you that you can inspect in person. Take an experienced friend along even if you're reasonably experienced yourself – two pairs of eyes are better than one when it comes to spotting crash damage or worn parts, and it's easy to talk yourself into a purchase if you're on your own with cash in your pocket.

Always remember the maxim: if it looks too good to be true, it probably is.

SIZING

Most reputable bike dealers will be able to help you with picking the right size bike. As with most large purchases it's worth getting a few opinions. For the standard cross-country riding position you are looking for comfort first and foremost, so feeling relaxed and being able to move freely are essential. The following is only a guide and, as everybody is

different, please make sure you seek personal advice from an experienced cycle fitter.

1 Stand-over height – the distance between the top tube and the floor – needs to be lower than your inside leg measurement so, should you have to step off the bike in a hurry, you won't have a nasty shock as your crutch smacks onto double-butted aluminium (ouch). You need about 2–3 inches minimum.

2 Reach – the distance between the handlebars and the saddle – is very important on a mountain bike. Your arms should be comfortably bent and the saddle-to-bar drop should allow you to sit with a relatively straight back. A shorter handlebar stem will quicken the steering and improve control, but being too cramped is uncomfortable on long rides and reduces climbing efficiency.

3 Correct saddle height is interpreted in a variety of ways. For optimum pedalling efficiency, the general consensus is that your leg should be slightly bent at the bottom of the pedal stroke, without your hips having to sway on the saddle to perform the stroke. Many riders choose to position the saddle slightly lower than this, compromising pedalling for better control over rough ground. It's an area that's open to interpretation, so have an experienced fitter check your saddle height.

4 Much of the fine-tuning of bike fit can be done by exchanging components such as the saddle and stem. Test ride the bike after each change and make sure you are happy with the setup before you leave the shop.

THE TEST RIDE

You may have to leave your credit card as security in the shop before they will let you out on a test ride. When you leave the shop, relax and take the bike for a gentle spin. Stop somewhere quiet and have a good look over what you are about to buy. If you aren't 100 per cent happy, don't feel pressurised to buy – try something else instead.

SELF-BUILD BIKES

In time you may want to have a go at assembling your own bike. Frame-only deals can offer excellent value, but be aware that used parts can create problems as you build. Things like front mechs and seat posts often vary in size and, unless you have all the right tools, you can easily make an expensive mistake. It's very rewarding when you're done, though.

BIKE BUYING TIPS

As with most things in life, there will be good and bad points about your new bike, but here are a few tips you should always consider before buying.

1 Research the brands you like the look of. Get hold of catalogues or visit manufacturers' websites to compare specifications and features.
2 Buy a range of up-to-date magazines to consider your options. Find group tests of bikes in your price range, or even e-mail the magazine to ask their opinion. Many magazines archive their tests online too.
3 When you're ready to visit a shop, take an experienced friend with you. They'll be useful both for advice and for spotting unhelpful sales talk.
4 Ask these questions at each shop you visit:
   • What size do I need and, if you haven't got it, can you order it in?
   • Can I have a test ride?
   • Do you provide a free first service?
   • Within reason, can I swap parts (saddle, stem, handlebars and so on) to get the exact fit I want?
   The answer to all of these questions should be 'yes'.
5 Consider that you will need after-sales support, so you'll need to build loyalty with the shop. Don't just buy more cheaply elsewhere and then expect a local dealer to fix or deal with the warranty on your new bike for free. It's always worth thinking about buying some extras (helmet, gloves, tools and so on) when you are at the shop buying your bike. This is probably the most you will spend in the shop at one time, so they may well offer you a few incentives even if it's just a free bottle and an inner tube.
6 Don't be lured by discounted bikes, special offers or ex-demonstration bikes unless you are absolutely sure it's the bike for you and it's the right size.
7 If the shop doesn't have your size, wait until they can get one. It's better to leave it a little longer and have the right bike.
8 Always ask local mountain bikers for recommendations and ask them about the local shops, for example which one is good for advice and which one specialises in particular brands, as it's always better to go to a dealer who has a good reputation. Ask lots of questions in the shop and make sure they have a good mechanic and a well-equipped (preferably tidy) workshop.

Rear shock

Shock linkage

Shifters

Stem

Headset

Brake levers

Suspension fork

Spoke

Tyre

Hub

Rim

Brake calliper

Disc rotor

Grips

Handlebars

Head tube

Brake hose

Gear cables

Front derailleur

Pedals

Crank arms

Rear derailleur

Saddle

Seatpost

Seat clamp

THE HOME WORKSHOP

Visit a good bike shop and you're likely to be impressed by the workshop facilities – the best shops have spacious, clean and comprehensively equipped workshops that you almost certainly won't be able to replicate at home. The good news is that you don't need to.

YOUR TOOL KIT

Professional workshops need to be able to deal with large numbers of bikes and handle anything that comes through the door. Your home workshop only has to cope with your own bikes, which massively reduces the amount of space and equipment you need. There are also a number of tools that it's generally not worth the home mechanic owning, and they tend to be the big, expensive ones. A shop might use, say, a frame facing tool several times a week – you might need one once in several years.

The best strategy with tools is to equip yourself with the most basic essentials first, which shouldn't cost too much – you can do a huge amount of work on a bike with just a set of Allen keys or a simple multitool. Add extra tools when the need arises – as your confidence builds and you tackle harder jobs, your collection of tools will grow appropriately. This approach spreads out your expenditure on tools and avoids the trap of acquiring expensive but rarely used tools.

We'd always recommend buying high-quality tools. They may cost a little more, but good tools last for years. Trying to undo stubborn bolts with cheap, soft Allen keys is frustrating and likely to end up with you damaging something on your bike or yourself. Specialist bike tools are expensive, but they make complicated procedures a breeze. Bodging jobs with cheap tools only ends in compromise, and if you have a good-quality bike it deserves the tools to complement it.

For a modest outlay you can cover most home workshop jobs. Frame tools, specialist tools and cutting tools do cost a fair amount, but in time you may consider them a worthwhile investment. In the meantime, the best advice is to buy components from a local shop and get their mechanic to fit them for you if you don't have the tools yourself. However, as you become a more competent mechanic you may want to consider how much you spend in the bike's workshop compared to how much the tools will cost you.

BASIC ESSENTIALS

These tools will get you started with simple cleaning and adjustment jobs. If you get nothing else, get these.

- Allen keys – 1.5,2,2.5,3,4,5,6,8 and 10mm are the sizes most often used
- Track pump
- Chain cleaner
- Cleaning brushes
- Pliers (flat and needle nose)
- Cable cutters
- Screwdrivers (small and large; flat and cross-head)

COMPREHENSIVE HOME TOOL KIT

As you progress to replacing parts, you'll need to extend your tool kit. These are tools to get as you need them.

- Nylon hammer (or mallet) and ball-peen (metal-working) hammer
- Metric, open-ended spanners – 8 and 10mm cover most jobs but it may make more sense to buy a full set
- Cassette lock ring tool
- Chain whip
- Cable puller
- 'Podger' – a sharp-ended tool like a bradawl
- Star nut-setting tool
- Adjustable spanner
- Cone spanners (17mm, 15mm and 13mm)
- Pedal spanner
- Workshop-quality chain tool
- Chain checker (for measuring chain wear)
- Torque wrenches
- Crank-removing tool
- Bottom bracket tools
- Headset spanners (if you have an old bike)
- Spoke keys
- Disc brake bleed kit
- Files (flat and half round)
- Socket set

THE TOOLS

1 Tool box
2 Long-nose pliers
3 Allen keys
4 Chainring nut spanner
5 Chain tool
6 Screw drivers

7 Chain whip
8 Pedal spanner
9 Cone spanners
10 Chain wear tool
11 Crank remover
12 Adjustable spanner
13 Cassette tool
14 Cable cutters

15 Tyre levers
16 Wheel jig
17 Crank bolt spanner
18 Torque wrench
19 Multi-tool
20 Shimano Bottom
Bracket tool

21 Star-fangled nut setter
22 Crank remover
23 Cassette tool
24 Cable puller
25 Spanner
26 Headset spanners
27 Cable pliers
28 Soft mallet

LUBRICANTS AND CLEANERS

You don't need specialist bike products for all cleaning and lubrication jobs, but it's easier to identify the right stuff that way and they tend to come packaged in more convenient quantities.

- **Ti prep (or copper slip)** – a grease with tiny copper flakes in it, which prevents titanium and alloys from seizing; this must be used on all titanium threads.

- **Anti-seize grease** – this is for large threads and components that stay put for long periods (seatposts, bottom bracket threads, headset cups and pedal threads).

- **PTFE (Teflon)-based light dry lube** – this is preferred for summer use and assemblies like derailleurs and brake calliper pivots.

- **Heavy wet lube** – this is best for wet weather as it's harder to wash away than dry lube.

- **Silicone greases** – use these for intricate moving parts like pedal and hub bearings.

- **Waterproof greases** – use these for components that get ignored for long periods like Aheadset bearings.

- **Degreaser** – used for cleaning moving parts and components that get bunged up with muck.

- **Bike wash** – this speaks for itself; use it for tyres, frame tubes and saddles.

- **Release agent** – this is good for removing seized seatposts and stubborn bottom brackets. Be careful as it can ruin your paintwork, and your skin.

A SELECTION OF LUBES AND GREASES – SEVERAL ARE NEEDED FOR DIFFERENT MATERIAL APPLICATIONS

WORKSHOP PRACTICES

PROTECTIVE EQUIPMENT

Lubricants, disc-brake fluid, degreasers and bike washes look after your bike well enough, but they can ruin your skin – always read the instructions and labels on cans before you start work. Take care and use appropriate PPE (Personal Protective Equipment) when working on your bike. Latex gloves and aprons are a great idea and safety glasses are a must when using release agents or operating grinders and drills. Using the right tools helps too.

LIFTING

Bikes aren't usually ridiculously heavy, but if you're dealing with freeride bikes (or tandems) they can be. It sounds daft to consider lifting a bike to be a hazard, but you'd feel pretty silly to put your back out putting your bike into a workstand. While it feels natural to pick up a bike by saddle and bars, you end up with your hands above your head – try crouching, picking it up by fork leg and seatstay, and standing up. The bike magically arrives at the workstand with your hands comfortably at chest height.

DISPOSAL OF HAZARDOUS SUBSTANCES

Hydraulic brake fluid and shock oils should be properly disposed of after use. Your local council tip will have a facility for dumping this stuff. DOT 4 and 5 brake fluids are very bad for the environment unless they are dealt with properly. Collect the waste in a clearly labelled container and find out where you can take it. Your local bike shop may also be able to dispose of it correctly for you.

READ THE INSTRUCTIONS

This may seem obvious, but it is very important. Warranties and guarantees are only any good if you install things correctly. Even the simplest of components will have some recommendations from the manufacturer – so stick to them. Use the recommended tools and torque settings.
If in doubt, contact the shop or the manufacturer. Don't make expensive mistakes.

DON'T FORCE IT

Bolts, bottom bracket cups, through-axles and other threaded parts and fasteners should screw easily into place until they start to tighten. If they don't, stop and find out why rather than seeking out a bigger spanner. You may have the part cross-threaded, or the threads may already be damaged. Remember that the threads in a bottom bracket shell or a post-style brake mount are usually formed in relatively soft material.

ADVANCED TOOLS

These are tools that you may never need but may be worth owning if you need them often. Weigh up the cost of tools against workshop charges and decide from there.

- Headset press
- Headset cup remover
- Crown race remover
- Crown race setting tool
- Thread taps
- Disc brake facing kit
- Steerer cutting guide
- Wheel dishing stick

PROFESSIONAL TOOLS

It's unlikely that these tools are worth a home mechanic buying, but don't let us stop you...

- Rear derailleur hanger straightening tool
- Rear dropout alignment tools
- Head tube reamer and facing kit
- Bottom bracket tapping and facing kits
- Fork crown facing kit
- Seat tube reamer
- Frame alignment tool
- Chainline gauge
- Spoke tension meter

WORKSHOP SET-UP

A home workshop is a bit of a luxury, but fixing your bike in the kitchen is never a great idea. So here are some bike storage ideas and tips for setting up your workshop at home.

1 A stable work stand is essential. The best workshop type will be fixed to a wall or a solid workbench, so jobs that require bashing or heavy leaning won't make the stand move around the floor as you 'dance' with your bike.

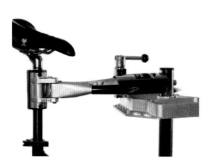

2 Put down a mat for spillage. Remember that if you have to fix your bike in the kitchen, you will need something on the floor to soak up the mess. Workshop mats are readily available from bike or tool shops. They also keep your feet warm in the winter.

3 Hooks and lockable anchor points are a good idea, just in case you are broken into. Storing your bike(s) like this also prevents them from falling over and getting scratched by the lawn mower.

4 A solid workbench makes tough jobs like fitting headset parts or cutting down fork steerers easy. A tool board helps you find tools quickly, and quality tools should be stored in a tool box if your workshop is damp. You can also assemble a field tool box that you can take with you to races or trail rides so you can fix emergencies in the car park.

5 The vice needs to be properly bolted and secured to the solid workbench. A vice is essential for hub and head-set jobs, and a pair of replaceable 'soft jaws' for the vice will help to protect valuable and sensitive components.

6 Your wheel jig should preferably be bench-mounted. A solid wheel jig makes truing wheels far easier. If you intend to learn how to build wheels, or just want to get better at home truing, then a wheel jig is a must-have item.

7 An electric drill will help with frame repairs and removing seized SPD bolts, and a bench-mounted grinder is useful for repairs and customising components, but care must be taken when working to wear the right PPE (Personal Protective Equipment).

8 Torque wrenches take the guesswork out of assembling aeroplanes, car engines and machines, and enable engineers to fasten bolts to manufacturers' recommended figures. This type is simple to use – set the level on the screw gauge on the handle shown in Newton metres (Nm), then add the correct Allen or bolt head (they have either a 3/8 inch or a 1/4 inch socket drive) and tighten the bolt until the handle 'gives' with a click. This type is perfect for most Allen bolts on a bike.

9 The Park Tools torque wrench has a beam, which 'bends' when the handle is balanced, allowing you to read off the torque on the dial. You'll need a bigger one like this for cassette lock rings, cranks and bottom brackets. On mountain bikes it is critical to use recommended torque settings, for warranty reasons and for safety – especially on suspension forks and disc brakes with many moving parts and fastenings. All well-trained mechanics will use a torque wrench – don't build a bike up without one.

10 Mountain bike tyres have a large volume and take a lot of air, so a track pump will set tyre pressures quickly and accurately and is far better than a mini pump. However, some pressure gauges are more reliable than others, so get a separate accurate tyre-pressure gauge too.

BEFORE YOU RIDE

Once you have bought your bike, it will be properly prepared and checked over by the shop mechanic (Pre-Delivery Inspection or PDI). The shop may ask you if you have any personal setup preferences, and they will also make sure that the gears are properly adjusted and the brakes are functioning safely. So, in theory your bike will be ready to take to the trails.

However, there are some things you may want to adjust when you get the bike home, mainly to suit your personal position on the bike and the controls, which the mechanic will have adjusted to a 'nominal' position. Nearly all mountain bikes now come with some form of suspension, which will need adjusting too. There are a number of simple checks you should make before setting off for a ride to ensure everything is secure and correctly adjusted. A couple of minutes spent checking before riding is time well spent. Always ask the shop to run through anything on the bike you are unsure of and never touch anything that may require an experienced mechanic – or wait until you have read the rest of this book!

FINDING THE RIGHT RIDING POSITION

If you've followed the advice in Chapter 1 you should have a bike that's the right size for you. Each size of bike is designed to cover a range of heights, though, so you'll still need to adjust the saddle, bars and controls to get the riding position spot on. There's a degree of subjectivity and personal preference to some aspects of riding position, but until you've worked out what your preferences are aim for a simple, balanced position. Get a friend to help you, take photographs or use a full length mirror to help you get the best balanced position.

SADDLE HEIGHT

Saddle height is one of the most important adjustments on any bike. It's slightly less critical on a mountain bike than on a road bike because of the different ways bikes are ridden. On a road bike you spend a lot of time seated and pedalling, on a mountain bike you're constantly moving between standing and sitting, pedalling and coasting.

The best rule of thumb for saddle height is that the knee should be slightly bent at the bottom of the pedal stroke.

An easy way to judge this is to adjust the saddle height so that your leg is fully extended with your heel on the pedal (while wearing the shoes you'll be riding in) at the bottom of the pedal stroke, with the crank arm in line with the seat tube. This should mean that when you put the ball of your foot on the pedal you have the appropriate slightly bent leg.

TOO LOW

With the saddle at the right height your upper legs will end up slightly below horizontal at the top of the pedal stroke. If your legs come up higher than that, your seat is too low for efficient pedalling and will put excessive strain on the knees. A very low saddle is great for steep, tricky descents but don't ride for prolonged periods like this.

Some riders choose to set their saddles very slightly (up to an inch) lower than the optimum pedalling height for a bit more clearance off-road, and if your riding involves a lot of out-of-the-saddle work that can be a useful compromise.

TOO HIGH

This often creates back problems as the rider will have to stretch to reach the pedals at the bottom of each stroke, which tilts the pelvis and pulls on the lower back muscles. The same principle applies if you bob back and forth excessively when riding hard as your back will tire and start to hurt. This is often why back pain is especially bad after a hard hilly ride or race.

SADDLE FORE/AFT POSITION

The traditional rule of thumb for fore and aft saddle position is that the centre of your knee should be vertically above the pedal spindle when sat on the bike with pedals level. Don't be too worried about getting this exactly right – it's a good starting point, but different riders have different preferences. Equally important on a mountain bike is the reach to the bars, which affects weight distribution and control. Don't be afraid to set your saddle slightly further forward or backward from the standard position for comfort or control.

ADJUSTING YOUR SADDLE

1 The seatpost should be greased regularly (unless it's made out of carbon fibre, for which a specific carbon-friendly assembly paste should be used). It's likely that you'll want to lower the seatpost out on the trail for long rocky descents and technical sections, which means you'll need to be able to move the saddle quickly. A seatpost can seize up very fast if you neglect to regrease it regularly.

2 The seatpost is held into the frame with a clamp, either with a quick-release lever or a simple bolt. To change the saddle height, simply undo the lever (or bolt), move the post to the appropriate height and retighten. If the seatpost slips, tighten the clamp more, but don't overdo it. If you're having to really heave on it, grease the cam section of the quick-release lever. If it's a clamp with a bolt, grease the threads and under the head of the bolt.

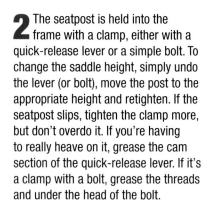

3 To adjust the fore and aft position of the saddle, loosen the clamp at the top of the seatpost that holds the saddle rails. This will vary depending on the style of seatpost – some have two bolts. With the clamp loosened, slide the saddle to your desired position and retighten.

COMFORT

Riding bikes off-road inevitably leads to some bumps and shocks, but it shouldn't be actively uncomfortable. It's worth spending some time getting your riding position just right to avoid putting unnecessary strain on your body – speak to your shop if you're struggling to get things right. You may need to change saddles if you can't get comfy on the one you have – there are many different shapes and widths available. Suspension bikes, either with just a fork or with rear suspension too, obviously help, but remember that your arms and legs are highly effective long-travel shock absorbers in their own right. A lot of comfort problems are caused by people being too tense on the bike. Bend your arms and legs, stay relaxed and let the bike move around beneath you.

4 The saddle should be level across the top – line it up with a brick wall or use a spirit level to check this. If you have a single-bolt seatpost you'll be able to tilt the saddle with the bolt loosened as for the fore and aft adjustment. Some seatposts have two bolts, one in front of the post and one behind. Loosening the rear bolt and tightening the front will drop the nose of the saddle and vice versa.

STEM AND BAR POSITION

The other key ingredients of bike fit are the stem and bars. The trend for most mountain bikes is for shorter stems (90mm or shorter) and wider bars (680-720mm is common), which give more control and a slightly more upright riding position. Even cross-country race bikes are going this way.

Usually your bike will have come with a bar and stem appropriate for the size of bike and intended use, but since one bike size covers quite a range of rider sizes you may need to change one or the other. Swapping the stem for one slightly shorter or longer can make a useful difference if you're at one end or other of the range, but be wary of changing to a stem more than 10-15mm different from the original. You're aiming for a balanced position, with weight evenly distributed between bars and saddle when seated.

BAR HEIGHT

Your weight distribution is also affected by the height of the bars relative to the saddle. Excessively high bars put your weight too far back, compromising the grip from the front wheel. Very low bars put your weight too far forward, making it hard to help the front wheel over obstacles in the trail and causing problems on steep descents. As a starting point, try the bars a couple of inches below the saddle (set at pedalling height).

STEM ADJUSTMENTS

Nearly every modern mountain bike has a handlebar stem that clamps onto the outside of the fork's steerer tube. To adjust the height you need to change the position of the spacers below the stem. See Chapter 12 for details. If there are no, or insufficient, spacers you'll have to change the stem for one that sits at a different angle.

HANDLEBAR ADJUSTMENTS

The other option is to change the handlebar itself. Bars are available in a wide range of rises – the difference in height between the centre of the bar and the ends where the grips are. Watch for the bar angle too – bars have sweep, for the best comfort they need to sweep up as well as back. See Chapter 8 for details.

POSITIONING THE CONTROLS

The final element of bike setup is positioning the brake and gear levers. These obviously need to be readily accessible for control, but beyond that there are many fine-tuning options that can improve things. Don't over-tighten the bolts on brake levers and shifters – they need to be tight enough to not move in normal use but allow them to move if knocked in a crash.

BRAKE LEVER ANGLE

The angle of the brake lever should be similar to the angle your arm takes to reach the handlebar; your wrists should be as straight and comfortable as possible when they are placed on the bars. This enables the tendons and muscles in your arm to pull in a linear motion, which is the most efficient way. It's worth experimenting with positioning the levers slightly higher than what appears to be the 'natural' position when seated – doing so promotes a dropped-wrist riding position which improves control. Higher levers are also easier to access when your weight is low and back for steep descents, which is when you need the brakes most.

Adjusting the lever angle is simple. There is a 4 or 5mm Allen bolt under the brake lever clamp. Depending on the particular levers and gear shifters used, the bolt can be tricky to access – ball-ended Allen keys that can be used at an angle are useful here. Or loosen the shifter first and move that out of the way.

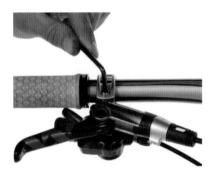

As well as the angle, you can adjust the levers in and out on the bar. Position them so that you can easily reach them with your first two fingers. Brake levers are also adjustable for reach – how far away they sit from the grip. This adjustment will either be a small Allen bolt behind the lever or sometimes an obvious tool-free dial.

SHIFTER POSITION

The gear shifters can be adjusted in the same way as the brake levers – loosen pinch bolt, move shifter, retighten. Position them so that you can easily reach the levers – SRAM shifters use only your thumb, Shimano ones use your thumb and first finger. The pods are designed to fit snugly to the brake lever, but be aware that the cable adjuster needs to be accessed easily – so don't rest it where you can't reach it.

The SRAM Matchmaker clamps shown here (Shimano has a similar arrangement) share a single bar clamp between the brake lever and shifter. The shifter can be angled up and down on the clamp and there are also two alternative mounting positions for in and out adjustment.

PRE-RIDE SAFETY CHECKS

There are a number of important, but quick, checks to make before each ride. The best pre-ride safety measure is to wash your bike after every ride (see pages 38-49). Washing your bike means you get up close to it, so you'll notice damage like cracks and dents and will also be able to inspect the derailleurs, chains and brakes for wear and tear. Always check anything usual, like noises and creaks.

Here are 12 safety checks that you should always carry out before setting off on a ride.

1 Frame. Frames don't last forever – they can get bent or suffer from metal fatigue and begin to crack. Look out for cracks around the welds, ripples or folds around the head tube and flaking paint, as they are all signs that the tube underneath has been twisted out of shape. If your bike has a steel frame, be aware of rust spots as these can be a sign of further damage on the inside of the frame tubes. See pages 175-177 for more on frame alignment.

2 Suspension fork. To check the fork action, apply the front brake and give the fork a few pumps – it should feel smooth, not sticky or notchy. Also note the rebound speed – if it is very slow there may be a loss in pressure or a spring failure. If it's extremely fast you may have lost damping oil. See pages 148-163 for more on fork setup and maintenance.

SUSPENSION SET-UP

If your bike has suspension, it will need to be adjusted for your weight. If you don't feel confident to tackle this, your shop will be able to help you – make a note of what settings they use so you can replicate them later. The bike manufacturer will also have recommended settings based on rider weight which are usually a good starting point. You can find out more about suspension setup on pages 148-163.

3 Rear shocks and suspension. Make regular inspections of the bearings and pivots. Keep the air pressure in the shock consistent to maintain the ride quality and place less strain on the moving parts. A depressurised shock out on the trail can damage the frame if you have to ride home, so consider taking a shock pump on the ride for emergencies, especially if you are going to be miles from home. See page 160 for more on rear shock maintenance.

4 Tyre pressure. All types of inner tubes and valves leak air gradually. Some lightweight tubes and tubeless tyres can lose as much as 20 per cent of their pressure overnight, so always check your tyre pressure. Use a workshop floor pump with an accurate pressure gauge if you can. Make a note of your preferred tyre pressure – the recommended range can be found on the tyre sidewall. Also inspect the treads for thorns, flints and glass, which may have become lodged in the tread. See pages 136-147 for more on tyres and tubes.

5 Wheels. Spin the wheels to check for smooth, quiet running and to ensure the brakes aren't binding. Grasp the top of each tyre and try to rock it side to side – if there's movement then the wheel bearings are likely to need adjustment or replacement. Lots of movement in the rear wheel could also be caused by worn or loose pivots in the rear suspension.

6 Brakes and headset. If you have disc brakes, make sure that there's reasonable lever travel – they're self-adjusting, but if the levers come back to the bars the pads are probably worn. If you have rim brakes, check for rim and pad wear visually – the pads have indicator lines in them and this is common on rims too. If your rims wear through they can split, which usually results in a nasty tyre blow-out. While you're pulling brakes, rock the bike slightly back and forth with the front brake on – any looseness here suggests that the headset may be loose. See Chapter 7 for more on brakes and pages 166-170 for more on Aheadsets.

7 Handlebars. Make sure that the handlebars are tight and check for bends or scratches. The basic rule is: if it's bent or scratched, bin it. Bends and scratches are both signs of fatigue – a bend will eventually snap and a scratch will act as a stress riser, which, given time and enough abuse, will eventually fail. See pages 106-108 for more on bar and stem setup.

8 Contact points. Contact points are where you rest your hands, feet and backside. They're all load-bearing and can loosen. Check the saddle fixing bolts on seatpost, seatpost binder bolt, pedals, crank bolts, stem and handlebar clamp bolts. Do not over-tighten, as over-stressed nuts and bolts are more likely to fail under impact. Use a torque wrench to check they are tightened to the manufacturers' recommended torque figures. See pages 104-115 for more on contact points.

9 Pedals. If you use SPDs or other clipless pedals, clean out your shoe cleats and retention mechanisms and lubricate the moving parts of the pedal. If it's muddy, spray some Teflon lube onto them to help shed mud. See pages 110-115 for more on pedal care.

10 Chain and cassette. Check the chain and cassette for wear and always apply fresh lube before you ride: wet oil for muddy and wet conditions and a dry Teflon lube for dusty summer trails. Clean the chain regularly too, as it will last far longer and shift better if it's not covered in dirt. Always run through the gears to check that they index properly and make sure all the cables move freely and aren't bent. See pages 50-63 for more on gear setup and pages 64-81 for more on chain and cassette care.

11 Front and rear wheel quick-releases.

Check that the front and rear wheel quick-release mechanisms are tight. If you arrive at the trail head in a car, chances are you will have to put the wheels back on the bike before you start riding, but if you don't it's worth double-checking that they are tight, especially if you use disc brakes. See pages 116-122 for more on removing wheels.

12 Tool kit and spares.

Once you're happy that your bike is sound, you're good to go. But don't forget to take your trail tools and spares with you. See page 178 for more on recommended trail tools.

04

CLEANING AND CHECKING

To keep your bike running smoothly and ensure that the components will last, wash your bike at least once a week – especially in the winter. Water gets into everything and therefore into all the sensitive parts of your bike, so it's best to wash your bike with care. Wear some wellies, rubber gloves and waterproof clothing, as you will then be able to concentrate on the job properly.

Pressure washers are certainly quick, but generally are not a good idea for cleaning your bike as they tend to blow water into sealed units such as the headsets, forks, hubs and bottom brackets. They also ruin your cables and blow all the lubricant off your chain. Worse still, with complicated full suspension linkages, which can easily be neglected, the water will quickly turn bearings to rust and seize up your pivots and bushings. So, it's far better to hand-wash your bike with a sponge and brush; this way your bike will last longer and perform better.

The other advantage of hand washing is that it forces you to get up close to the frame and components, allowing you to inspect them for wear or damage. The number of cracked frames that have gone unnoticed until the bike's been cleaned is beyond counting.

CLEANING YOUR BIKE

Find a suitable area to clean your bike. Be aware that you will need plenty of water and that the by-products from a mountain bike can be quite messy. Therefore, a concrete area with a water supply and a drain is best. Always clean the floor with a stiff brush when you have finished as the de-greasing fluids can make the floor very slippery.

1 Start at the top of the bike and work down, so you don't get muck on stuff you have already washed. If you're doing a thorough wheels-out clean then do the saddle and seatpost before putting the bike into a workstand.

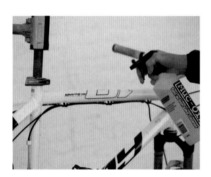

TOOLS REQUIRED

- **Water**
- **Bucket**
- **Variety of brushes (large to toothbrush size)**
- **Portable workstand**
- **Spray-on bike wash**
- **Strong degreaser (citrus ones are good) for drivetrain parts**
- **Sponge**
- **Chain-cleaning device**
- **Sprocket cleaner (narrow brush to get between gaps)**

2 Use a big brush and a sponge to get the worst of the mud off the frame and tyres. It's a lot easier to shift mud when it's wet, so clean your bike as soon as possible after riding. If you've been to a race or ride in the car, try to find space for a water container (or a garden sprayer) to get the worst off before setting off home.

3 Use a spray-on degreaser. You can dilute these cleaning sprays as they tend to be quite concentrated and powerful, and can even go 50:50 with many of them. Be careful to read the instructions as these fluids can be caustic and affect the finish of your bike – generally you don't want to leave them on too long before rinsing off. Most aren't too kind to your hands either, so it's best to wear rubber gloves.

4 You can (and should) use a more powerful degreaser on the chain, chainrings and sprockets. Because these are exposed, lubricated and low in the bike, they tend to get more gunged up than other parts. Removing wheels improves access, but it's easier to degrease the cassette and chain with the wheel in place – just spray the cassette and turn the pedals backwards to get the whole chain.

5 Use a small, stiff brush (an old pan brush is ideal if you don't have a bike-specific one) to clean the chain and sprockets. The idea is to agitate the degreaser so it works more effectively. Then get plenty of fresh water on the brush. Optionally, you can use a chain cleaner (see page 42).

6 Shift stubborn bits of dirt from between cassette sprockets either with a special tool as shown or with any stiff, narrow improvised tool – the edge of a rag or an old spoke works well. Every few cleans take the cassette off completely to clean behind it.

7 Fiddly bits like derailleurs and pedals are best tackled with a small, stiff brush that lets you get into all the little corners and gaps. A bottle brush, with bristles all the way around, is effective for the gaps between stays and tyres if you've left the wheels in.

8 Take care when cleaning disc brakes. Old chain oil or any kind of lubricant is bad for brake pads, so be careful about which brush you use and get some fresh water. Alcohol-based disc brake cleaning spray is effective.

9 Take similar precautions for suspension forks and shocks. They don't like water inside them, and while most degreasers sold for use on bikes won't harm the seals, it's safest to keep it away from them anyway.

10 Finish off by wiping down the frame with a soft cloth, and use a bit of water-displacing lubricant on the chain, sprockets, derailleurs and pedals. Relube the chain when it's dry.

USING A CHAIN CLEANER

While you can get perfectly satisfactory results by cleaning the chain with degreaser, water and a brush, chain bath cleaners are quick, easy and relatively clean.

1 Take the wheels out of the bike and place the chain on a chain retainer. This is a device like a dummy axle that positions the chain as if there were a wheel in place.

2 Clean in between the cassette sprockets and get all of the muck out of the jockey wheels on the derailleur. If you don't, the clean chain will get dirty again as soon as you replace the wheels and turn the pedals.

3 Fill the chain bath with a strong mixture of citrus degreaser and water and attach it to the chain. Different brands vary, check the manufacturer's instructions.

4 Hold onto the chain bath and rotate the pedals a few times to get a spotless chain – it's magic! Dispose of the used degreaser appropriately.

PRO CLEANING TIPS

1   If you're riding in really muddy conditions, spray the frame and drivetrain with extra spray lube such as GT85 or Shimano Chain Spray before going out. This will prevent the mud from sticking so much and means you can ride for a little longer before having to stop. Be careful not to contaminate disc brake pads when doing this.

2   Rather than a specific brush, use 1-inch strips of fabric to clean between the sprockets. T-shirt neck hems (the folded over bits) are particularly good for this job.

3   If you have to use a jet wash, ideally use it for the tyres, saddle and frame only. Wash the rest of the bike by hand. Stand back a bit when jetwashing, and be careful not to aim into the ends of bearings.

4   Use a bike wash detergent on all but the really stubborn muck. The concentrated and stronger degreasers (usually the citrus type) are best saved for the chains, chainrings and cassettes.

LUBRICATING

The modern bicycle's chain and gear system is finely tuned. Because all the moving parts of a bike transmission are external and open to the elements, it gets a fair amount of abuse. This assists in degrading and corroding all the moving metal parts. Basically, if you leave your bike out in the rain it will rust in a matter of hours, and if you leave the chain, suspension forks and rear shock covered in mud your bike will wear out pretty quickly. Lubrication helps prevent corrosion, but leaving a chain dirty and simply re-lubing it will just help attract more dirt. In the long term, this leads to a build-up of gunge and accelerated chain and sprocket wear.

The key to proper lubrication is to clean the component before you add any oil. Oiling an already mucky bike will just attract more muck, and cleaning components regularly will keep them running for a long time. Having followed the cleaning instructions on pages 40-42, it's time to relubricate before riding again. Only use bicycle-specific lubricants as some water-repellent sprays and lubricants have solvents in them that can damage the sensitive parts of your bike and ruin your paintwork.

WHAT LUBRICANT FOR WHERE?

JOCKEY WHEELS

Spraying thick lube all over the jockey wheels just attracts more crud to the chain and rear mech. If you have been riding a lot in wet weather, it's worth stripping the mech and regreasing the bushes inside the jockey wheels. See page 62 for more on replacing jockey wheels.

CABLES

Inner cables can be stripped out of the slotted cable guides and lubricated with a Teflon-based lubricant. A thin, light lube is best so as not to attract dirt. Many bikes now come with continuous cable housing which leaves fewer places for dirt to creep in. See pages 95-103 for more on cable replacement and servicing.

CHAIN

Clean the chain and use a dry lube in the summer and a wet lube in the winter or in wet weather. Use a water-repellent spray after washing and lube before every ride. See pages 64-69 for more on chain servicing.

REAR DERAILLEUR (OR MECH)

Use a thin lube on the rear mech and drop some oil onto the pivots. Work this in by running through the gears a few times. Check the spring inside the mech as it should be clean and rust-free. See pages 50-63 for more on gear servicing.

FRONT MECH

The more powerful spring in the front mech makes it less prone to sticking but the pivots will benefit from a drop of dry lube squirted and worked into the moving parts. Wipe off any excess with a rag. See pages 55-57 for more on front mech setup.

PEDALS

Clipless pedal mechanisms must be cleaned and lubricated regularly. They will bung up quickly if they are permanently dirty, so clean them if you've been riding (and walking) in mud. Clean the cleats in the shoes too as mud can get impacted into the soles and will prevent the cleats from releasing smoothly. See pages 112-115 for more on pedal servicing.

BRAKE LEVERS

Like any moving part, brake levers benefit from a squirt of lube to the pivot every now and again. If you're using cable-operated brakes make sure that the cable nipple can move freely in the cable-retaining hole. If this goes dry, the friction can damage the lever or break the cable. See pages 82-103 for more on brake servicing.

SHIFTERS

It's best not to spray lots of tacky gunge into these sensitive components. Lubricate them with a dry lube or light oil occasionally.

SUSPENSION FORKS

Never lubed your forks? Well, you should – a couple of drops of wet lube worked in with a couple of pumps on the bars will keep the seals sweet. See pages 148-163 for more on routine suspension servicing.

SUSPENSION BIKES

As with the forks, the rear suspension unit needs a drop of oil occasionally. The pivots and bushes also need a squirt of lube, especially after wet rides. See pages 148-163 for more on routine suspension servicing.

CANTI STUDS

If you're using rim brakes, spray a small amount of light dry oil behind the brake arm and onto the pivot. Obviously, do not spray the rims at the same time! Remove and regrease the studs on a regular basis as they are steel and will rust if exposed to lots of wet weather. See pages 82-103 for more on brake servicing.

TRACKING DOWN NOISES

Identifying the source of a noise requires a methodical approach. Try to narrow down the possibilities – if there's a creaking sound when pedalling, try standing up and sitting down to eliminate the saddle and seatpost as a cause. Try pedalling with one leg at a time. Some noises only appear when pedalling hard, but such noises could come from the bars or stem – you tend to haul on the bars when pedalling. If a noise doesn't go away when you're coasting, it's likely to be wheel-related rather than the transmission. Noises don't always come from where they sound like they do – frames are often good at transmitting sounds and making them appear to be emanating from somewhere else. Always check the simple things first – many noises can be cured just by tightening a loose bolt.

SQUEAKS AND CREAKS

A persistent noise from your bike can drive you mad. Squeaks, ticks and creaks can originate from many different places and they often need a careful process of elimination to find the source of the noise. Noises mean that there is something wrong so take them seriously. Take some time to track them down and sort out whatever it is.

The main cause of noise from your bike will be dry bearing surfaces or loose components. The friction between surfaces, whether at the threads in your bottom bracket or the clamp on your handlebars, will not be solved by spraying copious amounts of penetrating lubricant into the component – and in particular, don't do this to your handlebars as they could slip and cause a nasty accident. You can't always solve the problem simply by doing the bolts up a little tighter either, as they have recommended tightening torques and may simply need some anti-seize compound applying to them if they are titanium or aluminium. A persistent tapping can be something as simple as a cable end hitting the cranks as you pedal, or something less obvious like a broken chain roller, a worn freewheel or a loose hub. All the components should be checked for cracks or splits, and anything that looks unusual should be checked out and replaced if necessary.

SADDLE

The saddle is often the cause of pedalling-related noises. As the saddle is usually exposed to the muck off the rear wheel, it gets a lot of abuse and very little cleaning or care. The small shifts in weight across the saddle as you pedal cause movement in the rails, which can wear or start to work loose in the hull. The bolts in the seatpost can creak too. You may need a new saddle, or sometimes just removing it, cleaning everything, regreasing the bolts and reinstalling will quieten everything down.

SEATPOST

A dry seatpost will seize up pretty quickly. The residue and corrosion inside the seat tube can make a nasty creaking sound. Remove the seatpost and carefully clean inside the seat tube. Seriously corroded seat tubes will need reaming (cleaning out with a specialist cutting tool). Clean the seatpost with some wire wool and re-apply anti-seize grease (or assembly paste for a carbon fibre post) before you replace it.

SEATPOST CLAMP

Most frames have a separate seatpost clamp that pushes onto the frame. It needs to be a perfect fit and suitably tight. Seatpost clamps are also right in the line of fire of dirt from the rear wheel and need regular cleaning and regreasing. In particular, pay attention to the cam of quick-release clamps and the bolt in bolt-up clamps.

BOTTOM BRACKET

This is probably the biggest cause of pedalling noise. To solve any problems you'll have to remove it and at least clean and lubricate it. You may need to replace the bearings. See pages 72-79 for more information.

CRANKS

The traditional square-taper bottom bracket is often a cause of creaks and clicks, but that's now only found on old or inexpensive bikes. Most mid- to high-end bikes now use two-piece cranks with the spindle permanently attached to one crank arm – they're less susceptible to noise, but not immune. See pages 72-79 for more on removing and replacing cranks.

CHAINRINGS

Worn chainrings can cause all sorts of problems. As well as not running quietly, worn teeth can let the chain jump which is potentially dangerous. It gets worse with a new chain, too. Check for hooked or missing teeth and replace if necessary. See pages 80-81 for instructions.

CHAINRING BOLTS

These can often dry out and start to click as a result. Remove them, clean the cranks thoroughly and reassemble with anti-seize compound on the bolts.

CHAIN

This is often the cause of drivetrain noises. Stiff links can click or tap and are likely to cause skipping too. A very worn chain will make a graunchy rattling noise no matter how much lube you throw at it. Chain maintenance tips are on pages 66-69.

CASSETTE AND CASSETTE BODY

The cassette body is part of the rear hub and contains the freewheel mechanism. They don't last forever – a worn one will rock on the hub and may start to slip or stick. Either way it'll be making a bad noise by then. Flushing with light oil can get a few more miles out of them but it's usually a replacement job. Loose cassette lockrings, or loose screws holding cassettes together, can cause clicking or ticking sounds as well as affecting shifting.

REAR MECH

Squeaks are often associated with dry jockey wheel bushings. If the squeak stops when you stop pedalling, it's probably caused by either the pedals, bottom bracket or jockey wheels – these are the parts that rotate when pedalling. Badly adjusted gears will make a

whirring or clicking sound – check that the derailleur hanger hasn't been bent and thrown the gears out of line.

FRONT MECH

Very worn front mechs can rattle, and the sound is often amplified by the frame. Other common issues are clonking from the crank hitting a badly adjusted mech cage or ticking from the crank or your feet tapping a protruding cable end.

HUBS

Traditional cup and cone bearings need regular servicing, while cartridge bearings need periodic replacement. Both tend to deteriorate without you noticing until they get really bad. By the time they start making a noise, they'll be in need of serious attention.

PEDALS

Loose pedal bearings can cause creaks or clicks, while dry threads in the crank arms can cause creaks. Worn shoe cleats can be noisy too, and on some pedals the top plate can wear. Everything can be replaced, and often bearings can be sorted out with a strip and regrease.

HANDLEBARS

Handlebar creaks usually emanate from the front stem clamp due to loose or dry bolts. They need to have anti-sieze on them and be evenly tightened. But check the bar closely for cracks too – creaks are often the first sign of a broken bar.

STEM

As well as the handlebar clamp, stems have a clamp at the back to attach to the steerer and those can work loose or have dry bolts too. Other possible sources of creaking are the star-fangled nut inside the fork steerer tube or the top cap.

HEADSET

Dry bearings or broken races will make a very unpleasant creak as you pull on the handlebars. A strip and rebuild will usually eliminate the noise – re-pack the bearings with grease if you can, although cartridge bearings will generally need to be replaced. A badly adjusted headset will produce a knocking sound and a rattle that you can feel when riding. This can usually be adjusted out but if left too long may damage the headset. Very occasionally creaks come from the bearing races pressed onto the fork crown and into the frame. See pages 166-170 for headset adjustments.

SUSPENSION FORK

Many suspension forks make twanging, gasping, or other noises even when in perfect working order, so you're listening for new or different ones. Hissing can be a sign of a damaged air seal, while coil forks can break springs and make a scratching sound. Both of these will affect the fork's performance too. Knocking sounds can be caused by worn bushings between the fork stanchion and slider, although they could also be from the headset.

REAR SUSPENSION

The same noises that afflict forks can be made by rear shocks, too. A common issue is clicking or knocking caused by worn shock bushings. Rear suspension pivots can all work loose or wear out too.

BRAKES

The most common brake noise is the dreaded squeal. Many disc brakes squeal under certain conditions, but if they squeal all the time check for contaminated or glazed pads, or loose bolts on the calliper or rotor. Very worn disc pads will whirr, and if you get down to the metal they'll screech. Whirring could also mean a bent or broken pad return spring interfering with the rotor. General rubbing or dragging sounds are usually the result of a mis-aligned calliper, warped rotor or simply the wheel not being in quite straight.

WHEELS

Loose spokes can make plinking or clicking sounds as they move against one another at the crossing point. Disc brakes put different loads on wheels to rim brakes, and often braking will highlight loose lacing. Retensioning should sort it out.

05

GEAR SYSTEMS

A wide range of gears is one of the defining characteristics of the mountain bike, although as mountain bikes have become more specialised the gear range has often come down – downhill race bikes don't need low gears, and bikes ridden for fun rather than racing can get away without high ones.

The number of sprockets on the rear wheel has been going relentlessly upwards over the years. The original klunkers had just one, then five or six when derailleurs were grafted on. The mid-1980s saw the arrival of indexed gears, with one lever click giving one gear. Seven speeds at the rear became the standard, then eight, nine and now ten (with eleven starting to appear).

Front shifting is indexed too, although increasing numbers of bikes are coming with just two chainrings rather than the traditional three. More sprockets at the back means you can have a wider range without big jumps between gears, and you can get almost as wide a range with two chainrings as used to be the case with three. Doing away with a chainring saves a little weight, improves ground clearance and is easier to set up.

Fitting more sprockets into the same width (the overall width of a ten-speed cassette is the same as an eight-speed one) means narrower sprockets, more closely spaced, with narrower chains. This means that ten-speed systems are more particular about alignment and adjustment than earlier, more forgiving, setups.

REAR DERAILLEUR

Indexed gears work by the shifter pulling just the right amount of cable per click to move the derailleur across one sprocket. It's a surprisingly reliable system considering the conditions that it has to work under, but you'll occasionally have to make small adjustments to the cable tension as the cable stretches. You'll have to set the tension correctly if you replace the cable, too. Derailleurs also have adjustable end stops to prevent them shifting the chain off the cassette, and these will need setting up if you've fitted a new derailleur.

1 Different mechs have the limit screws in different positions, but they'll all have two located close to one another and labelled H (for High) and L (for Low). Shift into the highest gear (smallest sprocket) and make sure that the H screw prevents the chain from moving any further. If the chain comes off the small sprocket it can get jammed in the gap between sprocket and dropout.

TOOLS REQUIRED

- **Cross-head screwdriver**
- **5mm Allen key**

2 Similarly, adjust the limit screw marked 'L' when the gear is in the largest sprocket (lowest gear). Don't worry too much about the indexing working too well at this point, as you need to set the throw of the mech before tweaking the gears. Double check that the chain can reach this sprocket, but also that the chain cannot jump over the top of the cassette and into the wheel. Also check that the mech cannot hit the spokes of the wheel. This can have disastrous consequences, so it is essential that you make sure this cannot happen.

3 With the limit screws correctly set, move on to the indexing. Hold the back wheel off the ground in a workstand, leaving your hands free to pedal the bike and adjust the cable tension. Tension is adjusted using either the barrel adjuster on the mech itself, where the cable enters the body, or – if you have one of the many current derailleurs that don't have a barrel adjuster – the one on the shifter.

4 Start by running through each gear and listening for any noise as you change up the gears, going from the smallest cog to the largest one. Check how easily the chain moves across the gears – if it struggles to make the next largest sprocket then the cable is too loose, so you will need to tighten the cable by turning the barrel adjuster anti-clockwise. Now shift across the cassette from large to small sprocket. If there's a delay in the shift or if the chain stays stuck in one gear then the cable is too tight and you will need to loosen it by turning the adjuster clockwise.

5 You should be able to adjust the cable such that shifts are clean and immediate in both directions. If the shift is still bad it may be due to one of the following problems:

- The gear hanger is bent (see page 175 for frame alignment).
- The chain is too long or too short.
- The cables are old or dirty, or there is a kink or obstruction somewhere in the run.
- The chain or sprockets are worn out.
- The cable is clamped into the rear gear in the wrong place.

6 The final check is the angle adjustment screw. This controls how far below the sprockets the upper jockey wheel sits, and needs to be set for different cassettes. Shift into the largest sprocket at the back and small chainring at the front. Adjust the screw so that the upper jockey wheel is just below the sprocket. Too close and it'll bump into the sprocket, too far away and shifting will suffer. Turn the screw clockwise to increase the clearance, anti-clockwise to reduce it.

RAPID RISE

Traditional rear mechs are sprung outwards – left to their own devices they'll shift to the small sprocket, with cable tension pulling them towards larger ones. For a brief period Shimano manufactured Rapid Rise (or 'low normal') derailleurs that were sprung towards the large sprockets and used cable tension to pull them towards smaller ones. They didn't prove popular. If you encounter a low normal mech, the principles of cable tension adjustment are exactly the same but reversed.

COMPATIBILITY

When replacing shifters and derailleurs, you need to ensure that you get compatible parts. Shimano and SRAM rear derailleurs and shifters aren't generally interchangeable due to the shifters pulling different amounts of cable and the derailleurs being designed accordingly. SRAM does manufacture a range of Shimano-compatible shifters, although they're not common. You also need to match the number of clicks in the shifter to the number of sprockets to ensure that the derailleur moves the correct distance per shift – 8, 9 and 10-speed cassettes all have different sprocket spacing. Derailleurs themselves are quite accommodating, with 9-speed mechs working happily on 8-speed setups. Ten-speed units are designed to operate with larger sprockets and you may have issues with chain width due to narrow cages and jockey wheels. Front mechs are interchangeable between brands but again 10-speed units have narrow cages that can cause rubbing with 9 or 8-speed chains. Double-ring specific front mechs with a smaller radius cage are also available and work better with two chainrings.

FITTING

1 The rear mech needs to be installed onto the gear hanger. Check that the hanger is straight and that the threads are clean and uncrossed. The rear gear has to hang perfectly straight. If the hanger is bent or the derailleur cage is twisted, the system will not work. Most aluminium and carbon fibre frames have replaceable hangers. If you have a steel frame with a bent hanger it'll need to be straightened – see page 175.

2 The chain has to be threaded through the jockey wheels. If there's a chain already fitted (perhaps because you're replacing a worn or damaged mech), refer to page 68 for splitting and rejoining. If you have a Shimano chain, or a SRAM 10-speed one, it may be easier to remove the bottom jockey wheel from the mech to avoid disturbing the chain.

TOOLS REQUIRED

- **3 and 5mm Allen keys**
- **Small pliers**

---

3 Make sure the shifter is in the small sprocket position. Feed the gear cable inner wire into the hole in the mech and clamp it under the washer and bolt on the mech body. To see how this works, look for a channel moulded onto the body of the mech – the washer will be marked where the cable has been. If the cable is clamped to the wrong side of the bolt, shifting will suffer.

CLUTCH MECHS

Newer derailleurs from SRAM and Shimano feature clutch mechanisms in the upper pivot that make it harder for the mech cage to swing forward. This helps the mech to maintain tension on the chain and reduces chain clatter and the likelihood of bouncing the chain off over rough ground. Shimano's Shadow Plus

mechs have a lever to turn the clutch on or off – it's easiest to turn it off when removing the wheel or working on the mech.

---

4 Screw the gear barrel adjuster fully in, so that there will be plenty of adjustment available when setting the cable. If all the cable outer sections are properly inserted and the gear shifter is in the highest gear position, it should be possible to pull the cable tight enough with your hand. Pull the cable in the direction of the channel you have identified in step 3. Lock it off with the clamp bolt. Follow the instructions on page 52 to set up and adjust the mech.

FRONT DERAILLEUR

Front shifting is in some ways more forgiving than rear. The more powerful spring in a front mech means that it's better able to deal with a little bit of cable drag, and with a maximum of three chainrings to accommodate, indexing is less critical. Twin-ring setups are even easier. The main challenge is alignment. Direct-mount front mechs that attach to a specific tab on the frame are becoming more popular and guarantee good alignment, but the traditional mech that clamps around the seat tube needs a little more attention for optimum performance.

BASIC ADJUSTMENT

1 Angle the mech so that it is exactly parallel with the chainrings. When you buy a new front mech it should have a small plastic spacer inside the mechanism. Do not pull this out as it is there to help you set the position and height of the mech. It allows you to align the outside plate of the mech cage with the outer (biggest) chainring and position the mech over the middle chainring. If you don't have the spacer because you're adjusting an already installed mech, a little more trial and error will be needed to position it.

TOOLS REQUIRED

- **Small cross-head screwdriver**
- **5mm Allen key**

2 If the angle is slightly out (as shown here), the shifting will be sloppy, so make sure you set the angle carefully. Spend time getting this bit right as it will have the biggest influence on the performance of the mech. If it is angled too far outwards it will foul on the crank when the pedals are turned, making a clonk with each pedal revolution. Shifting will also be poor and you'll get chain rub in some gears.

3 The vertical distance between the outside mech plate and the teeth of the chainring should be no more than 2–3mm. This will ensure that the mech is correctly positioned to

cope with the difference in size of the granny (smallest) ring and big ring. It also allows for the chain pick-up and will happily clear the teeth of the chainrings.

4 A good chainline is imperative; make sure that the chain can access all of the rear sprockets when in the middle chainring. You can also see that the mech in this position is exactly in line with the outer (big) chainring. With the cage correctly aligned, you can remove the spacer from the mech.

5 Adjust the limit screw marked 'L' first. Place the rear mech in the biggest sprocket (lowest/easiest gear), as this is the furthest the chain will travel. Then set the front mech so that the chain only just clears the inside of the cage plate. In the granny ring you will probably only use three or four of the lowest gears, so make sure that these are working properly.

6 Next, attach the gear cable. Make sure that the gear shifter is in its lowest position so the cable is at its slackest, and set the barrel adjuster on the shifter a turn out from fully in to give you room for adjustment. In this position the front mech will be over the granny ring. Pull the cable through the clamp firmly. Trap the cable in the clamp and check that it's in the right place, as this can affect the shift. Once the cable is pulled through and set you can adjust the low-limit stop screw.

7 Check that the chain shifts cleanly between the inner and middle (or inner and outer if you have a double-ring setup). If it doesn't want to shift to a larger ring, tighten the cable slightly by turning the barrel adjuster anti-clockwise. If it's hesistant to drop back to a smaller ring, loosen the cable. When you're happy, check the middle ring to big ring shift in the

same way. It shouldn't need further adjustment – if you can't get into the big ring you may need to adjust the high limit screw.

8 Put the chain onto the big chainring and work the rear mech through all the gears. You will notice that the chain changes angle considerably, but it will cope with most of the gears on this chainring. Set the limit screw so that in the smallest rear sprocket it just clears the chain.

9 On some full suspension bikes this adjustment can be very tricky. Here the rear swingarm is in the way of the adjustment screws, so you would need to use a longer screwdriver.

FITTING

1 Having obtained the correct replacement mech (see 'Getting the right front mech', right), you'll first need to remove the old one. Most front mechs have a screw holding the back of the cage together – removing this allows you to get the chain out of the cage, saving you from splitting the chain. If the front mech is riveted together then you'll have to break and rejoin the chain – see page 66.

2 With the chain free, loosen the cable pinch bolt and release the cable. Then undo the mounting clamp and remove the old mech. You're likely to be able to see clearly where the old mech was from marks on the paint. This is a good starting point for positioning the new mech. Bolt it on, thread the chain through the cage (either by splitting the chain or removing the cage screw) and then follow the 'Basic adjustment' instructions.

GETTING THE RIGHT FRONT MECH

There is a huge number of variations in front mechs, so you need to take care to get the right one. Traditionally, front mechs clamp around the seat tube of the frame, which may be one of several diameters. Many front mechs come with a set of shims to accommodate any diameter, but some are size-specific. If you're replacing an old mech, the size should be stamped somewhere on it, often inside the clamp. Clamp-on mechs will either be low or high mount. Low-mount mechs have the parallelogram mechanism above the clamp and are also known as top-swing mechs. High-mount mechs have the parallelogram hanging down from the clamp and are also known as bottom-swing. Most hardtail frames will accommodate either, but full suspension frames tend to require one or the other in order to clear parts of the suspension. Direct-mount mechs that bolt straight on to a special threaded mount on the frame are becoming increasingly popular and make alignment easy.

The final option is the direction from which the gear cable comes. It can either be routed under the bottom bracket and approach the mech from below (bottom pull), or along the top tube and approach from above (top pull). Most mechs can work with either by using built-in cams, but some will only work with one kind of routing. Check before you buy.

Top pull and bottom pull – both these mechs are bottom swing

A top swing, direct mount mech

CAUSES OF FRONT MECH RUBBING

If your front mech is rubbing, it will be due to one of the following problems:

1 The cable is too tight or too loose.

2 The limit screws are incorrectly adjusted.

3 The angle of the mech cage to the chainrings is wrong.

4 The chainline is incorrect.

CAUSES OF UNSHIPPING A CHAIN

If you have problems with the chain unshipping, it will be caused by one of the following:

1 The low adjust is set incorrectly, so you will have to push the mech further out with the limit screw.

2 The chain is jumping over the top of the biggest chainring, so you will need to push the mech further in with the limit screw.

REPLACING GEAR CABLES

Gear cables are the one element in the gear system that must be friction-free at all times. To keep a smooth-running gear cable you need regular check-ups and plenty of lubrication. Replacing the cables regularly will make your bike shift better and protect the levers from extra wear and tear. The gear cable outer has to be in top condition for the index system to work properly, so always check the cables after crashes as they are very brittle and vulnerable to cracking.

The secret to good cabling is a very good-quality (sharp) set of cable cutters. Only use your cable cutters for cables, not for spokes and small bolts! The easiest way to measure outer cable lengths is to use the old bits of outer cable as cutting templates. The cables should be long enough that they don't snag or pull taut when the handlebars are fully rotated. Over-long cables flap about, which is both inefficient and dangerous.

Gear cables are thin (1.2mm) and flexible, with a small nipple on one end. Don't confuse them with thicker brake cables. Recalcitrant shifting can often be sorted out simply by replacing the inner wires, and it's worth trying that before replacing the housings as well – inner wires are very cheap.

REPLACING INNER WIRES

1 Inner wires have to be threaded into the shifter first, then routed to the mech. The nipple on the end of the cable is pulled by the shifter mechanism in one direction, while the spring in the mech pulls the cable back the other way when released. Shimano RapidFire shifters have a cross-headed plug covering the cable access hole.

2 Put the shifter into the highest gear position by clicking the release lever (the smaller, upper lever) repeatedly. With the cable plug removed, the internals of the shifter should now line up so that the cable can be fed through the access hole, emerging at the barrel adjuster. Feed it through all the housing and replace the cable cover.

3 Some SRAM trigger shifters also have a cable port, but many require you to remove the shifter cover. This is secured by either one central bolt, or three at the edges. Some current SRAM units can be detached from the bar clamps and this can make access easier.

4 With the cover off and the shifter clicked to the highest gear, the cable routing will be obvious. Remove the old cable and feed the new one in through the mechanism and out through the barrel adjuster. As with Shimano shifters, feed the cable all the way through the housing and replace the shifter cover.

5 The third common style of shifter is the grip shift. SRAM made its name with grip shifters, although Shimano has some budget units that are found on entry-level MTBs and hybrids. The principle is the same as for other types of shifter – click into the highest gear position, remove the cable access cover, pull out the old cable, push in the new.

6 Check all the lengths of housing as you thread the inner wire. Cracked or split housing, or missing or damaged ferrules can all hinder shifting. It's also worth fitting small O-rings to exposed cable runs to avoid them clattering on the tubes.

7 Route the cable to the appropriate mech (don't get them back to front – the shifter on the right of the bars is for the rear mech), feed it through the cable stop and secure with the clamp bolt. Adjust the shifting as described in this chapter.

8 Once you're happy with the shifting, give an exposed bit of cable a good yank to make sure all the housings are fully seated in the stops and to get the first bit of cable stretch out of the way. Re-adjust the shifting as appropriate. Cut off any excess cable and crimp on an end cap to prevent fraying.

REPLACING CABLE HOUSING

1 Proper cable cutting is the first step in making your gears work properly. Gear cables have a very brittle plastic outer casing, which can be damaged or cracked by using the wrong cutters when cutting them to length. Use cable shears that slice through the cable rather than pliers or cutters that just crush the casing.

2 The gear cable is different from the brake cable in that it is made up of strands that travel the length of the cable, inside which is a nylon liner that the gear cable can run through. These strands are very hard and cannot be compressed, so they transfer all the effort from the gear shift into bracing the inner cable (or wire). This pulls on the derailleur and in turn pushes the chain onto the next sprocket or chainring.

3 Cutting the outer cable crimps the cable liners, closing up the hole that the inner wire has to go through. Use a bradawl or a podger to make the hole in the liner big enough for the inner wire to pass through unhindered. This reduces the friction on the cable and enables you to run the inner wires through easily once the cable ferrules are in place.

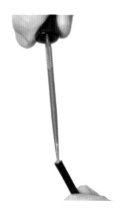

4 Outer cable ferrules must be applied to the end of each cable outer run. Cables without ferrules will fray and crack at the ends and the cracks will travel up the cable, which doesn't do much for your gear shift and allows water to get into the cable. Eventually, the cable strands will push their way through the cable guides and the whole system will pack up. Plastic ferrules don't rust and are less likely to seize into the cable guides.

5 Outer gear cable runs should change direction as smoothly as possible. Any tight angles will apply pressure to the inner wire and therefore add friction. This slows the shift and can cause the gears to jump. On suspension bikes it is especially important to make sure that these runs are unhindered and have enough space to move as the bike moves. Check that the bars can turn freely without being hindered by cables.

6 Apply a small smear of grease to the ferrule before you push it into the cable stop or guide. This will make it easier to adjust the cable at the derailleur and also prevent it from getting stuck or seized up.

7 There is a seal on the final run of cable to the rear derailleur. This is designed to prevent water from running down the cable and into this very sensitive area. Unprotected sections will allow water in and eventually rust the inner wire and dry the outer cable so that the whole lot seizes up.

9 On traditional mechs with the cable entering from the rear, the final run of outer needs to be long enough to allow the rear derailleur to travel across all the gears – the body of the mech swings as it shifts, and there needs to be enough cable to accommodate this without having a huge loop of outer.

11 Many bikes now use continuous runs of housing all the way from the shifter to the rear mech, rather than short lengths between stops and exposed runs along straight sections. This is partly to keep dirt out and partly because a lot of bikes have very few straight tubes.

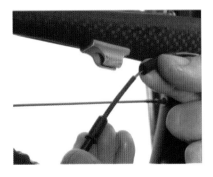

8 Slotted cable guides enable the cables to be completely separated from the bike. This makes lubrication and inspection of the inner wire easy. To release the cable, place the derailleur in the lowest gear (on the largest sprocket at the back). Then stop pedalling and release the shift lever completely. This will send the cable completely slack, allowing you to release the cable outers from the guides.

10 Shimano Shadow and SRAM derailleurs route the cable from the front, negating the need for the near-180° loop that traditional mechs use. They do need a precise length of housing between the last stop on the frame and the stop on the mech.

12 Remember to protect the frame and the paintwork from the outer cables as vibrations from the trail will cause the cable to wear away at the frame. Place frame stickers where the cables rub, particularly by the handlebars but also at any point where a cable touches the frame. These sticky protectors will protect the cable from wearing through too.

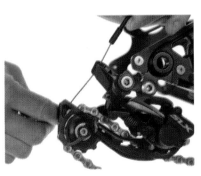

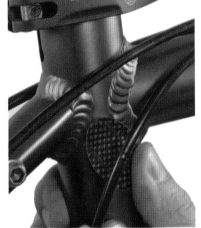

JOCKEY WHEELS

1 Rear mechs work best with free-running jockey wheels. These can be replaced when the plastic wheels wear out. This improves shifting and helps keep the chain in contact with the sprockets on the cassette.

2 To replace the jockey wheels, remove the pivot screws. However, if you haven't done this before it's worth paying attention to how it goes back together. Take a photo of the mech from both angles if you are in doubt before you remove the bolts. The bush should be in the centre of the wheel.

3 This is the bottom jockey wheel from a Shimano XT rear mech. The bushes are made from a ceramic material so they do not rust up. The top jockey wheel has a sealed bearing in it. It is worth stripping and reassembling both wheels. Clean them completely and reassemble, using a Teflon lubricant.

OTHER CABLES

Mountain bikes are increasingly sprouting cable-operated parts other than gears. Remote lockouts for front forks or rear shocks are a common example, while remotely operated telescopic seatposts for on-the-fly saddle height adjustment are growing in popularity.

Most of these use essentially the same cables as gear systems, and all the same maintenance and replacement procedures apply.

4 Make sure that the jockey wheel is replaced so that it rotates in the right direction. There is usually an arrow on the plastic part of the wheel to help you do this. Once you have reassembled the cage, check that the top and bottom fixing screws are tight.

06

DRIVETRAIN

Even strong riders don't generate much power compared to engines, so it's vital that the bicycle transmission is as efficient as possible. Bikes have been using chains and sprockets to transmit drive for as long as there have been bikes, and while other systems have been tried (toothed belts are getting a lot of attention at the moment) nothing's yet been found to better it.

The modern drivetrain is, of course, considerably evolved from 100 years ago, offering smooth and highly efficient power delivery – lab tests have shown bike chains to be 98-99% efficient under ideal conditions. Of course, a mountain bike transmission rarely operates under ideal conditions. It's exposed to the elements, with mud, grit and water all conspiring against it.

As a result, it's vital to take good care of the transmission. Regular cleaning and checking for wear (see Chapter 4) is a must. All parts of the transmission – chain, chainrings, sprockets and bottom bracket – should be considered consumable, though, and will need regular replacement.

CHAINS

Bicycle chains are incredibly efficient, but have to put up with a lot of abuse, and the constant twisting and shifting up and down the sprockets wears the average mountain bike chain out in a matter of months. A combination of good gear technique, constant chainline and regular care will prolong a chain's life. Look at a singlespeed bike – chains that don't move from side to side will last years rather than months.

There is also a variety in the quality of chains. Plated chains are the best, as they are less likely to corrode and therefore last longer and shift better than a plain steel chain. Stainless steel chains are also available; they last a little longer than plain steel chains but, as they are harder, they can wear aluminium chainrings if they aren't regularly cleaned and lubricated.

As the chain wears, the distance between the links gets longer. This is commonly referred to as stretch, although it's not really stretching – the pivots and bushings at each link are getting thinner. The cassette sprockets wear as the chain does, eventually reaching the point where a new chain will skip on the old sprockets or chainrings. To avoid having to replace the entire drivetrain, replace chains often. Using a cheap chain and replacing it often – rather than buying an expensive chain and waiting until it wears out the sprockets and chainring too – will turn out cheaper in the long run.

TOOLS REQUIRED

- **Chain checker or ruler**
- **Quality chain tool**
- **Pliers**
- **Grease**

REGULAR CHECKS

1 Measure across 12 full links of the chain (24 pins) with a steel rule. A new chain will measure 12 inches (chains are made in inches, so it's easiest to use inches for this measurement). If it's less than 12 1/16in there's plenty of life in it. Replacing a chain at 12 1/16in usually means that the sprockets and chainrings will be fine with the new chain. If it gets as far as 12 1/8in the sprockets will be quite worn and may skip. Beyond 12 1/8in, skipping with a new chain is almost inevitable.

2 Chain-measuring devices, like the Park one pictured here, are simple to use although less accurate than a ruler. Simply hook one end into the link and use either side to ascertain how much stretch there is in the links. In this case, the gauge will not slot into the corresponding link as the chain is brand new. A worn chain would allow the peg to drop between two rollers. The numbers refer to percent elongation – 1.0% is 1/8in across 12 full links. The 1/16in 'safe' point is 0.5%, so if you reach 0.75% on the Park checker it's time to replace the chain.

3 You can also assess the state of the chain and the chainrings with a quick visual check. Put the chain on the biggest chainring and smallest cassette sprocket. If you can pull the chain off the chainring and it can clear the tip of one of the chainring teeth, or the chain moves excessively at the top and bottom of the chainwheel (demonstrated here at the front derailleur and crank arm), there is some chain wear and it should be replaced.

4 There are many ways of getting a bike chain the correct length. Too short and you won't be able to reach all the gears. Too long and shifting will be poor and jumping is likely. The rear derailleur cage should be exactly vertical when the gear is placed in the highest combination (big chainring and small sprocket). If you are replacing a chain, check that this is the case before you remove the old chain.

CHAIN TROUBLESHOOTING

- If a new chain jumps or skips, it's likely that the cassette or chainrings are worn. Commonly used sprockets wear out faster. On triple chainsets, the middle chainring is usually more heavily used than the others – you may be able to get away with just replacing that one (see page 70).

- If a chain breaks, it was either incorrectly joined or worn out. It's a good idea to carry a reusable joining link on rides to get you home in the event of a broken chain, but we'd recommend replacing the chain as soon as you can.

- Chain suck usually happens when you shift to extreme gear ratios for climbing and are placing a lot of pressure on the pedals. This gets worse as the chain wears out. Hooked and worn chainrings also affect chain suck as the chain 'sticks' to the chainrings and gets jammed between the frame and the chainset. The best solution is to keep components clean and replace them often, before chain suck happens.

5 This is the biggest spread of sprocket to chainring that is possible. You can see that the chain is pulling the rear derailleur at a very extreme angle. Some mechanics use this position to measure the chain, placing the new chain around this chainring/sprocket combination and adding two links to allow for the derailleur. Some full suspension systems move the rear axle further away from the bottom bracket as they

compress – do this check with the rear shock deflated or unbolted at one end to allow for this.

6 Ideally the derailleur also needs to be able to take up all the slack chain in the small chainring/small sprocket combination. With a triple chainset and a very wide gear range this may not be possible, although you'll only be using the three or four largest sprockets when in the inner chainring.

REMOVING AND JOINING SHIMANO CHAINS

Originally chains could be split or rejoined simply by pushing one rivet out with a chain tool and then pushing it back in again. The demands of multi-speed derailleur gears and narrow chains means that this is no longer possible. Shimano chains use a special non-reusable joining pin. Make sure you get the correct chain for your bike. They're different widths for different numbers of gears, and must match – a 10-speed transmission needs a 10-speed chain.

1 This flat-ended pin marks the spot where the chain was first joined. You can break the chain anywhere except at this pin. Remove the old chain and, assuming that it was the correct length, measure the new one next to it. You'll usually have to remove a few links from one end. Thread the new chain through the rear derailleur jockey wheels, front mech cage and over the chainrings. Rest it on the bottom bracket for now.

2 Leaving the chain off the chainrings will give you some slack and make it easier to re-join the two ends. The special Shimano joining pin has a narrow, pointed part to make sure that the link is pushed in the correct way. You need a pin that's the right width for the chain you're joining – 10-speed ones are narrower than nine.

3 Push the link through using a quality Shimano-compatible chain-tool. This Park tool has shaped jaws to prevent the side plates becoming squeezed together. Keep the chain straight and turn the handle firmly and slowly to make sure that the pin goes through straight.

4 You need to push the pin right through so that the pointed end comes out of the other side of the chain. You'll feel a slight click as the pin reaches the right point. Back off the handle of the chain tool and check that the fatter part of the pin is equally spaced on either side of the link plates.

5 Once you're happy that the pin is in the right place, snap off the pointed end by gripping it with pliers and twisting it off. It will snap cleanly off. With the guide pin broken off, you can run the bike through the gears and make sure everything is working.

6 If the chain jumps, the freshly joined link may be slightly stiff. To remove a stiff link, first add some lube to it and push it into an inverted V shape. Then place your thumbs on the links to either side of this link. Grip the chain and gently push the chain against itself. This very careful 'bending' should free the link immediately.

SRAM AND OTHER CHAINS

1 Rather than a special joining pin, SRAM chains use a joining link. Eight and 9-speed links are called Power Links and are reusable. Ten-speed links are called Power Locks and can only be used once – they need a chain tool to remove. You'll need to shorten the chain to the right length in the usual way but ensure that you remove the side plates – the Power Link/Lock joins the chain between two rollers. Joining a Power Link or Power Lock involves pushing one link pin through each roller, pushing the two plates together so the pins go through the holes and then pulling the ends of the chain apart so it clicks shut.

2 There's a bit of a knack to removing Power Links. Take the tension off the chain (it's best to lift the chain off the chainrings first), squeeze the side plates and push your hands towards one another at the same time. KMC chains use a similar joining link, and also offer a 10-speed reusable link that can be used on Shimano chains. If you're really struggling with removable links, special pliers are available to make opening them easier.

CASSETTE SPROCKETS

All but the very cheapest bikes have the freewheel mechanism integrated into the rear hub (known as a freehub), with the sprockets in a cassette that slides on to the hub and is secured by a lockring. Even if the cassette doesn't need replacing, it's worth removing periodically to clean behind it. You'll need to remove it to service the hub, too.

When replacing cassettes, make sure you get the appropriate part. The Shimano-pattern freehub has become an industry standard, so 8, 9 and 10-speed cassettes and hubs from all manufacturers are generally interchangeable. Seven-speed cassettes use the same spline pattern but the freehub is narrower, so cassettes with more sprockets won't fit (and you'll need a spacer to fit a 7-speed cassette onto an 8-speed freehub). SRAM's 11-speed system uses a different freehub body. You need to get a cassette with the same number of sprockets as the one you're replacing, unless you're upgrading, in which case you'll need new shifters too (and possibly other parts).

Cassettes are available in a huge range of sizes. You need to get one with the same number of sprockets as before unless you want to change your shifters too.

TOOLS REQUIRED

- **Cassette lockring tool and spanner**
- **Chain whip**

1 Remove the cassette using a chain whip and a cassette-removing tool. The chain whip prevents the cassette from turning, and should be positioned so that the chain on the tool can wrap around the sprocket enough to prevent it from spinning when you push on the wrench.

2 The lock ring threads into the cassette body and secures the sprockets. Because the cassette is integral to the drive, it needs to be tight. The serrated teeth pressed into the last sprocket and the underside of the lock ring prevent it from vibrating loose.

3 The first two or three cassette sprockets will be loose, so be careful not to drop them. Lay the wheel flat on the work-bench and take the sprockets off one by one, placing them down in the order in which they came off the wheel.

4 Once the loose cassette sprockets and washers have been removed, the main cassette cluster can slide off. There is a series of slots cut into the cassette body. These are shaped so that the sprockets can only be returned the right way around.

6 Lastly, replace the cassette cluster, the washers, the loose sprockets and the lock ring. Then tighten the lock ring to 35–50Nm. You'll be surprised how tight this is, but the cassette bears a considerable load and needs to be checked for tightness regularly. If you don't have a torque wrench, it's a decent push with a 12in spanner – you should hear a number of clicks from the lockring.

5 Apply a thin layer of grease or anti-seize to the cassette body before you slide the cassette back into place. This will prevent the cassette body from rusting as water can get into the cassette very easily. If there is any corrosion on the body, use a fine wire brush to clean it off. A brass suede shoe brush is good to have in your tool kit for this type of job.

CRANKS, CHAINRINGS AND BOTTOM BRACKETS

Most frames still have a traditional threaded bottom bracket shell into which the bearings thread. Early MTB bottom brackets used adjustable cup and cone bearings with loose balls that required attention even after the smallest rain fall and needed the patience of a bird watcher to set up without play or dragging. These were superseded by the one-piece unit with sealed bearings and a fiddle-free cartridge housing. These are simple to fit and can be left alone until worn out. Cartridge bottom brackets are available with a range of axle types. Square taper axles have been around for a very long time and still work as well as ever. The quest for a stronger, stiffer interface led to the introduction of ISIS and Octalink units with larger, splined axles. These mount to the frame in the same way as square taper units – the only difference is the way in which the cranks attach. Some cartridge bottom brackets have adjustable lockrings that allow you to vary the position of them across the frame to tune the chainline.

The downside of ISIS and, to a lesser extent, Octalink is that the larger axle means smaller bearings (because they still have to fit inside the bottom bracket shell). ISIS in particular gained a reputation for poor durability. The most common style of bottom bracket at the moment is the outboard bearing type (Shimano

TOOLS REQUIRED

- **Crank puller and spanner**
- **Torque wrench and 8mm Allen socket**
- **Vice or large spanner**

Hollowtech II, Race Face X-Type, SRAM GXP and others). By positioning the bearings outside the bottom bracket shell on the frame, these systems can use a stiff, strong 24mm axle and have large bearings too. The bearings still thread into the frame, but the axle is permanently attached to one crank arm which is pushed through the bearings after installation.

Growing numbers of bikes are appearing with unthreaded bottom bracket shells. There are a number of variations, although they all use bearings that push into a plain bottom bracket shell – a little like a headset on its side. Pressfit bottom brackets use the same cranks and axle as outboard bearing systems, but the bearings are housed in plain carriers that push into either side, with a flange to stop them going too far. The BB30 standard uses a larger-diameter shell to accommodate a 30mm axle. BB30 bottom brackets are literally a pair of bearings that are pressed directly into the shell, located by either steps inside the shell or circlips in grooves. Pressfit 30 uses the same crankarms as BB30 but has the bearings in carriers as per the smaller Pressfit standard.

Chainsets or cranksets are the engine room of the bike – that is, the bit that gets all the power directly from your legs and helps you rip up the trail. They consist of three main components: the crank, the chainrings and the spider.

Q FACTOR

This is the distance across the pedal faces, which dictates how far apart your feet end up. A wide Q factor is bad because all your joints have to compensate; your knees get especially abused and bend the wrong way with a wide Q factor. Mountain bikes typically have wider Q factors than road bikes, although the increasing prevalence of narrow-profile double chainsets has redressed the balance slightly.

CRANK ARMS

The crank arm has to be really stiff – this is an absolute priority. Stamping and pulling on a strong crank relays all the power you can muster to the rear wheel, while flexible cranks are inefficient and are more likely to break unexpectedly. Their shape should be smooth and flowing, and there should be no sudden changes in shape or section. Sharp pockets and cut-out areas cause stress raisers and cracks to start, leading to eventual breaks. Modern two-piece chainsets with 24 or 30mm hollow spindles are noticeably stiffer (and often lighter) than traditional designs.

Crank arms are available in different lengths, although 175 and 170mm are the commonest sizes, with others being rarer. The one you use is up to you – there are no set rules – but will also be governed very slightly by your leg length: 175mm cranks give better leverage but aren't ideal for riders shorter than 1.7m. Most manufacturers will put 170mm crank arms on small bikes for this reason.

REMOVING AND REPLACING CRANKS

OUTBOARD BEARING, PRESSFIT AND BB30

1 Removing modern two-piece chainsets is very straightforward, but there are a few variations in how they work. Shimano chainsets have the axle permanently fixed to the drive-side crank arm. To remove the left-hand arm, first loosen the two opposing Allen bolts.

2 With the bolts loosened, you'll be able to undo the plastic preload cap using the Shimano TL-FC16 tool (other tool companies make

compatible tools, but the simple plastic Shimano one is all you need). Some Shimano cranks have a stopper plate in the clamp slot – flick this upwards to disengage its pin from the hole in the axle.

3 The left-hand crank should now pull off by hand. It may take a bit of waggling to loosen it from the splines on the axle. If it really won't shift, make sure the bolts are loose and that the stopper plate is disengaged. If everything is loose, a gentle tap to the back of the arm with a rubber mallet should pop it off.

4 With the left-hand crank removed, the right-hand crank and axle can be pulled out. Some Shimano chainsets have O-ring seals on the axle next to the bottom bracket bearings – be careful not to lose these. The axle may need a gentle tap on the exposed end with a rubber mallet to free it from the bearings.

5 SRAM chainsets come in two versions. GXP models are very similar to Shimano, with the axle permanently attached to the drive-side crank and the left-hand crank fitting onto splines on the end of the axle. The main difference is that the left-hand crank is secured by a bolt that threads into the end of the axle, like an old-style bottom bracket. The bolt is held behind a cap so that undoing the bolt with an 8mm Allen key pushes the arm off the axle. With the arm removed, the axle and drive-side crank pull out in the same way as Shimano units.

6 SRAM chainsets with 30mm axles for BB30 and Pressfit 30 bottom brackets work the other way around, with a 10mm Allen bolt on the drive-side that pushes the right-hand crankarm and chainrings off the axle. Depending on the exact setup, there'll be various spacers and shims on the axle – take careful note of the order these are in so you can put them back correctly.

7 Be sure that you attempt to undo the correct crankarm on a SRAM chainset. The non-removable arm may have a tempting-looking bolt head, but this should not be undone. If you're not sure, take a close look – the non-removable bolt should have 'Do not remove' engraved on it.

8 In all cases, refitting is the reverse of removal. Make sure that all the spacers are in place on the axle, and use a rubber mallet to seat the side of the chainset that carries the axle into the bearings – use tape to protect the face of the crankarm. Place the removable crank arm onto the splines. SRAM cranks need tightening to 48-54Nm, which is substantial; 30mm units have a preload adjuster behind the crank which needs adjusting until it contacts the bearing face. For Shimano cranks, tighten the preload cap finger tight, then do up the pinch bolts alternately to 10-15Nm.

SQUARE TAPER, ISIS AND OCTALINK

1 The traditional bottom bracket setup has the axle and bearings as one unit, with a crankarm fitting on each end (rather than the axle being permanently attached to one or the other and the bottom bracket just being the bearings). Usually the fixing bolt has an 8mm Allen head with the washer as an integral part of the bolt and an integrated plastic dust cap. Older cranks will use a 14 or 15mm hex-headed bolt and washer protected by a separate dust cap.

2 Unlike two-piece chainsets, traditional units won't just pull off by hand (unless they're broken). You need a crank puller to pull them off the bottom bracket axle. The puller screws into the extractor threads that will be revealed once you've removed the bolts and washer. Clean out any

mud from the crank threads with a squirt of spray lube. Undo the centre bolt of the puller, then thread the outer part into the crank. Make sure it goes in straight. ISIS and Octalink cranks require a larger head on the crank pulling tool – a puller designed for a square taper axle will just go inside the larger splined axles.

3 Once you have correctly inserted the puller, tighten the plunger. The tool shown has an integrated handle, some pullers have a hex head that you'll need to turn with a spanner. The arm rests on the end of the axle and the pushing/pulling motion forces the crank off the square axle taper. Make sure the outside part of the puller is fully inserted. If you strip the extractor threads in the crank you'll need to replace it.

4 Keep hold of the crank otherwise it'll fall on the floor when it comes off the axle. Remove the crank puller and repeat the procedure on the opposite crank. With both cranks off you have access to the bottom bracket. This is an ISIS crank – Octalink cranks are similar but the spline pattern is very different. Don't mix them up.

5 To refit, clean the splines on the ends of the axle and the inside of the crank and apply a smear of grease. ISIS and Octalink cranks have a stop on the axle so the cranks always go on by the same amount. It's still a good idea to use a torque wrench to tighten them correctly.

OTHER OUTBOARD BEARING CHAINSETS

Various other manufacturers make outboard bearing chainsets similar to Shimano and SRAM systems. FSA and Race Face are two brands that you're likely to encounter, but there are many others. They all go together similarly, with variations on which crank comes off and how it's secured. The instructions above cover most setups, but check the manufacturer's instructions if you're not sure.

6 Some mechanics suggest not greasing square tapers, but some lubricant means you get consistent tightening for a given amount of torque. All the grease will be forced out of the crank/axle interface as you tighten it.

CHAINLINE

For ideal shifting you really want the chain to be at its straightest in the middle chainring (on a triple) and in the middle of the cassette, allowing for optimum spread of gears with less chain angle. This improves shifting, prolongs the life of the chain and prevents it from unshipping unexpectedly. In practice, the chainrings are usually slightly more outboard than this in the interests of frame clearance. Double chainsets should align the centre of the cassette (between two sprockets on 8 or 10-speed) with a point halfway between the two rings. This chainline tool lets you check the alignment, although modern bottom bracket systems make it hard to get it wildly wrong.

REMOVING AND REPLACING BOTTOM BRACKETS

With the crankarms out of the way, the bottom bracket itself is accessible. The majority of modern bottom brackets, whichever type they are, are essentially non-serviceable and are simply replaced when worn. Some high-end internal cartridge units have replaceable bearings, though – it's worth checking before replacing the whole lot. It's also possible to replace just the bearings in many outboard bearing units, but while this can save some money it's a bit awkward and not recommended by the manufacturers. Outboard

FRAME PREPARATION

All frames must be properly prepared before you attempt to fit a bottom bracket. Bearings and cups must run parallel and threads must allow you to fit the bracket without forcing it with a tool. Cross-threading bottom brackets can be a costly mistake, so if you are in doubt get an experienced mechanic to prepare and fit the bracket for you – ask to watch them do it and you'll learn for next time.

TOOLS REQUIRED

- **Shimano C-spanner TL-FC32 (supplied with bottom bracket)**
- **Shimano axle-bolt tool TL-FC16 (supplied with bottom bracket)**
- **Allen keys**
- **Torque wrench**
- **Grease (Shimano Anti-Seize is good)**

BBs are relatively inexpensive and easy to fit anyway.

Whether square taper, ISIS or Octalink, all internal threaded bottom brackets are removed and fitted in the same way. The same is true for outboard bearings, although again they're not necessarily cross-compatible with different chainsets (see right).

OUTBOARD BEARINGS

1 To remove an outboard bearing, use the appropriate C spanner – this is a Shimano one, most tool brands have their own version – to unscrew it. Remember that the right (drive) side has a left-hand thread and unscrews clockwise. The left (non-drive) side has a conventional right-hand thread.

2 With the bottom bracket shell empty, make sure that it's faced on both sides. If the faces of the shell aren't parallel and flat, the bearing housings could become distorted or misaligned when fully tightened. You will find that some frames need more preparation than others. Clean out any swarf from the bottom bracket and use some anti-seize grease on the threads.

3 Depending on the width of the bottom bracket shell, you'll need spacers for correct spacing and chainline. Measure the width of the bottom bracket shell – it will be either 68mm or 73mm. 68mm shells require two spacers on the right and one on the left. A 73mm shell requires one spacer on the right. If you have a bottom bracket mount front mech or chain device, that takes the place of a right-hand spacer – on a 73mm shell there would be no spacers, just the mech or chain device plate.

4 Fit the internal plastic cover to the right (drive) side cup and thread it into the bottom bracket shell. Remember that the drive side is a left-hand thread (tightens anti-clockwise). Screw it in finger tight – if it won't turn easily, make sure it's not cross-threaded. Repeat for the non-drive side cup. Finally use the C spanner to tighten both cups to 35-50Nm and refit the crank arms.

BOTTOM BRACKET COMPATIBILITY

While the various brands of outboard bearing bottom bracket look the same, they're not interchangeable. Shimano and Race Face systems use 24mm axles, but SRAM uses a stepped axle that's 24mm on one side and 25mm on the other and can only be used with specific bottom brackets. FSA cranks also use 24mm axles, although it's safest to stick with FSA bearings – there are sometimes tolerance issues that mean a poor fit with Shimano (or compatible) units. Aftermarket manufacturers like Hope make bottom brackets for all systems.

CHAIN DEVICES

Originally the exclusive preserve of freeride and downhill riders, chain devices to hold the chain securely on the rings are increasingly popular on trail bikes. 1x9 or 1x10 setups don't have a front mech, so a chain device is essential to stop the chain unshipping from the ring. There are a number of roller-style devices that work with double chainsets too, increasing tension on the chain and wrapping it further around the rings. The best of these devices use a mounting plate that bolts to special tabs on the bottom bracket shell – the ISCG (International Standard Chain Guide) system. If your frame lacks ISCG tabs, you'll need a guide that mounts behind the drive side bottom bracket cup. With outboard bearing bottom brackets, remove one of the spacers from behind the drive-side cup (the only spacer if it's a BB30 or Pressfit 30 BB). The mounting plate will take its place.

SQUARE TAPER, ISIS AND OCTALINK

1 Most conventional bottom brackets use the same splined tool to remove and refit, although ISIS and Octalink units need a tool with a larger hole in the middle to accommodate the bigger axle. Undo the non-drive side first – this is usually a separate removable cup. Turn the tool with a ratchet handle or large spanner, taking care not to let it slip in the splines. Repeat for the drive side. Remember that the drive side unscrews clockwise.

TOOLS REQUIRED

- **Bottom bracket tool**
- **Ratchet handle or large spanner**
- **Torque wrench**
- **Callipers or ruler (for measuring bottom bracket and shell)**
- **8mm crank Allen key**
- **Anti-seize compound or synthetic grease**

2 Clean out the frame's bottom bracket shell thoroughly with a degreaser and dry it off. Then dress all the threads with plenty of anti-seize or quality synthetic grease. The bottom bracket is often neglected for many months, so how easy it is to remove depends on how well it was prepared before it was put in.

3 The new unit will have one removable side, which is usually on the non-drive side. Pull this off so that the unit can be installed into the drive side first. This side has a left-hand thread and tightens anti-clockwise. If the threads have been properly prepared, you will be able to turn the unit with your fingers. Spin it in until there is about 1cm of thread left. You will now be able to insert the non-drive-side cup. This tightens clockwise and will mesh with the cartridge inside the shell. Most Shimano brackets have a taper on the

inside that allows them to self-locate. Again, tighten this with your fingers until there is about 1cm of thread left showing.

4 Use the bottom bracket tool to tighten the unit into the frame. Make sure that the shoulder of the unit on the drive side is tight up against the frame first. This is to make sure that the chainset will sit in the right place and that it will not loosen off. Once the drive side is tight you can tighten the non-drive side. Tighten both cups to 40–50Nm, then refit the cranks.

BB30 AND PRESSFIT

BB30 and Pressfit bottom brackets, with an oversized, unthreaded bottom bracket shell, need the old bearings to be drifted out with a specialist tool and the new one pushed in with special adaptors on a headset press. While it's entirely possible to use improvised tools, the possibility for expensive frame damage means it's a job best left to a shop. If you already have a headset press, though, it's exactly the same procedure as replacing press-in headset cups – see page 171.

AXLE LENGTH

Cartridge bottom brackets are available in range of lengths, with the traditional square taper unit coming in the largest number of different sizes. ISIS and Octalink come in just a few. The axle length you need will depends on the crank you're using and the width of the frame's bottom bracket shell – wider shells need wider axles so that the cranks clear the frame. When you replace a unit, always use the same length axle. Shorter axles can mean that the chainrings rub on the frame, while longer ones will mess up your chainline and your gears won't work. If you are fitting a new crank and bottom bracket, check with the manufacturer which length axle you will need to match your old setup. Switching to an outboard bearing setup makes things easy – they're all the same width (except for specialist freeride and downhill versions designed to work with extra-wide rear axles) with spacers behind the bearings to allow for different shell sizes.

CHAINRINGS

Chainrings come in hundreds of sizes and are made in a variety of manufacturing processes: stamped, CNC-machined and sometimes part-cut, part-machined. Most chainrings feature an array of ramps, pins and cutaway teeth to assist the chain in shifting, although unramped chainrings for single-ring applications are widely available – many riders are taking advantage of the availability of super-wide-range 10-speed cassettes to switch to a simpler 1x10 system with a single ring up front.

The advent of 10-speed has meant that double ring setups are becoming commonplace on new bikes. With a wider range of gears at the back, it's possible to achieve a sufficient spread of gears with two rather than three chainrings, saving weight and simplifying setup. You can convert a triple to a double simply by replacing the outer chainring with a bashguard, but specific double chainsets have the rings moved across for better chainline and will have more appropriate chainring sizes. A typical triple has 22/32/42, while a double may have 24/36, 26/39 or various other combinations.

Chainrings mount to the spider with a number of bolts, arranged in a circle. The diameter of the circle through the centre of the bolts is called the pitch circle diameter (PCD) or bolt circle diameter (BCD). Different cranks have different BCDs, and there are now a lot of variations. Make sure that replacement chainrings have the

TOOLS REQUIRED

- **5mm Allen key**
- **Chainring peg spanner**

correct BCD. Don't be afraid to experiment with ratios, though.

The other thing to watch is that chainrings have got thinner as the number of sprockets at the back has gone up – more sprockets means a narrower chain and hence thinner chainrings. Usually wider chains work happily on narrower rings (eg an 8-speed chain on a 9-speed ring) but the reverse isn't always the case.

CHAINRING BOLTS

Chainring bolts are made from steel, titanium or aluminium, depending on your pocket. Steel bolts are probably the best as they are cheap and strong. They need greasing every now and then as they can seize if left to rust. Use copper grease on the bolts. Titanium bolts are very light but very expensive, and also require special attention if left for long periods of time as they can seize up. Use plenty of copper slip or anti-seize compound on them and only tighten to the manufacturer's recommended torque setting. Aluminium bolts are really light but not very strong and can snap off. Chainring bolts take a 5mm Allen key and should be tightened gradually and in sequence (that is, not from left to right but from opposite bolt to opposite bolt) so that you don't over-tighten them and to ensure that the rings run true. There is

one set of chainrings for the two large (or one larger, in the case of a double) chainrings and one set for the inner ('granny') ring.

REPLACING CHAINRINGS

1 It's possible to remove and replace chainrings with the crankarms mounted on the bike – they can be wriggled out over the crank spider. However, modern chainsets are so easy to remove that you might as well do so. It makes it a lot easier to get at the inner chainring bolts. Undo these with a 5mm Allen key.

2 With the bolts removed, the inner ring can be lifted off. You'll need to take the inner chainring off even if you're only aiming to replace the middle or outer. When mounted, the inner ring blocks access to the sleeve nuts for the bigger rings.

3 The bolts for the outer chainrings undo from the outside. Be very careful not to cut your hand on the outer chainring as the bolts come loose. With a bit of thought you can orient the Allen key so that you can squeeze it towards the crank arm.

5 With all the bolts and sleeve nuts removed, the two outer chainrings (or one chainring and a bashguard, or just the big ring if it's a double chainset) will come free. Twist the outer chainring so it clears the mounting tabs and lift it off.

7 It can be a little fiddly getting the outer two chainrings together. Once you've got one bolt in the rest are easier. Use anti-seize grease on the bolt threads and on the outside of the sleeve nuts. This will make them easier to shift next time. Tighten the bolts in a crosswise fashion, not round in a circle.

4 If you're lucky, the sleeve nuts will stay put and you'll be able to unwind the bolts from the other side. If the nuts spin, you'll need to use this special wrench to hold them via the slots in their outer face.

6 When replacing the rings, pay attention to the orientation. The ramps and pins must align correctly for optimum shifting. The outermost ring will have a peg on it that should go behind the crank. The others will have a nub on the inner circumference that also aligns with the crank.

8 Some cranks have detachable spiders, allowing different ring sizes (or a single ring with integrated spider) to be fitted. Different cranks need different tools for the spiders – this one uses a Shimano lock ring tool.

07

BRAKING SYSTEMS

Mountain biking in tricky terrain is all about control, and a lot of that control comes from your brakes. Brakes aren't just about stopping. Successful off-road riding depends on being able to modulate your speed, and the more steep and technical the trail the more important that is.

Brakes have come a long way since the Californian klunker pioneers. Their earliest bikes used coaster brakes in the rear hub, activated by putting backwards pressure on the pedals. The famous Repack descent was so-called because the riders had to strip and re-grease their coaster hubs each run – they would boil out thanks to the heat generated by the brake.

Cantilever rim brakes from touring bikes were quickly adopted, with motorcycle brake levers adapting them for flat, rather than dropped, bars. Cantilevers stuck around until the mid-90s when Shimano's V-brake was launched. The power and ease of setup of the V-brake meant that it became ubiquitous very quickly.

The next big development was the introduction of disc brakes. There had been a number of disc brakes in small-scale production in the early 1990s, but it wasn't until the later years of the decade that discs became mainstream. Once standards for rotor and calliper mounts were established there was no stopping them. Discs took braking away from the rim, made it more consistent, less affected by weather and requiring less adjustment. Today only the very cheapest mountain bikes come with rim brakes – the vast majority of modern frames and forks don't even have bosses for them. Entry-level bikes tend to come equipped with cable-operated discs, which have many of the advantages of disc brakes but are still affected by contaminated cables. Hydraulic disc brakes use fluid in hoses to push the pads onto the rotor.

BRAKE PADS AND TYPES

New disc brake pads should be bedded in before riding them in anger. This burns off any residual resin from the pad and ensures that it's properly mated to the brake rotor. It's a simple process – find a quiet road, ideally going

---

TOOLS REQUIRED

- **Needle-nose pliers**
- **Allen keys**
- **Flat-blade screwdriver**

---

downhill, and do several hard stops from a reasonable speed. After ten or so you should feel the brake lever getting firmer and the brakes becoming more powerful.

ORGANIC PADS

Organic brake pad compounds are made from a variety of materials – rubber, glass, aramid fibres and so on. They provide good stopping power and modulation but work best at lower temperatures. They also generate less heat than sintered pads, but also wear faster. Note that some brake rotors are designed for use only with organic pads.

SINTERED PADS

Sintered pads are made with metallic compounds to create a harder pad. They're more effective at higher temperatures and last longer, making them a better bet for winter conditions. They generate more heat than organic pads, which some brake systems don't appreciate – check the manufacturer's recommendations. The harder pad may also cause premature wear on rotors not designed for them. Such rotors usually carry a warning – check before buying new pads.

PAD CARE

Always remove your pads before bleeding your brakes or doing

anything else likely to contaminate them. Take care when cleaning your bike not to get degreasers or lubricants on the pads. Don't pull the brake levers with the wheels out of the bike – the brake will try to adjust for a rotor that isn't there and end up with the pads wedged together, requiring you to lever them apart before refitting the wheel. Use a spacer in the calliper to stop this happening if you take the wheels out for transport.

REPLACING DISC BRAKE PADS

Once fitted and aligned, hydraulic disc brakes require little maintenance beyond keeping them clean. The most frequent task is replacing the pads. Brake pad lifespan is affected by numerous factors – pad compound, soil type, riding style, weather conditions and more. A set of pads could last for months, or they might be destroyed in a single day. It's a good idea to carry at least one spare pair of pads on rides just in case the latter occurs – they don't take up much room. Check pads regularly for wear. The best way to check is visually, but you'll get warning signs when riding. Hydraulic brakes self-adjust as the pads wear, but only up to a point. If the brake lever starts getting closer to the bar, it's probably time for new ones. Eventually you'll wear through all the friction material and the metal backing plates will contact the rotor. This is both noisy and ineffective. It'll also damage the rotor.

We're using Shimano brakes here, but the principles are the same for most brakes. Note that brakes from different manufacturers use differently shaped pads – those for an Avid brake won't fit a Shimano brake, for example. You can't guarantee that pads are interchangeable within brands, either. There are a number of different shapes to fit various Shimano brakes, so take care to get the right one.

1 Remove the wheel (see page 118). Pads are held into calipers by some form of retaining pin. It may be a threaded pin that unscrews, sometimes with a c-clip on one end to stop it coming loose. Or, as here, it may be a simple split pin. Split pins usually have the end bent over to keep them in, so straighten that with pliers first.

2 With the split pin straightened (or c-clip removed) pull out (or unscrew) the pin. It will usually pass through a tab on each brake pad, as well as the pad return spring sandwiched between them.

3 Hydraulic brakes self-adjust for pad wear, which means that the pistons will be too close together to fit new pads. To retract them, use a broad, flat-bladed screwdriver to gently lever the old pads apart. The old pads will protect the pistons. Cable-operated discs will need to be adjusted out manually.

4 The pads and spring will simply lift out of the caliper. Squeeze them together and pull. On these Shimano brakes they come out upwards – some brakes require the pads to be taken out downwards, it's usually obvious which it is.

5 Assemble the new pads and spring. The prongs of the spring should sit either side of the friction material on the pad, resting on the backing plate. Some brakes have handed pads, on others it doesn't matter.

6 Push the new pads and spring into the calliper, making sure they go fully home. Some brakes have internal clips or magnets to hold the pads. Replace the retaining pin – if it won't go in, the pads aren't inserted correctly. Put the wheel back in and pump the brake lever a few times to reset the callipers.

FITTING BRAKE ROTORS

Brake rotors don't need replacing very often, but they do wear out eventually. They last a lot longer if you refresh your pads regularly and keep the callipers and rotors clean. You're more likely to have to replace one because it gets bent. Remember that the rotor-to-pad spacing is around 0.5mm so it won't take much of a buckle to mess it up. You'll also need to remove them to service your hubs and it's a good idea to take them off if you're packing your bike into a box to travel so they don't get damaged. There are two mounting standards for MTB brake rotors.

SIX-BOLT ROTORS

1 The most common rotor fitment is the six-bolt type, using six equally spaced bolts to secure the rotor to a flat face on the end of the hub shell. Make sure that the rotor is oriented correctly on the hub. There'll be a rotation arrow marked on the rotor.

TOOLS REQUIRED

- **T25 Torx driver or 3mm Allen key**
- **Threadlock**

2 This Shimano rotor uses anti-rotation washers to help prevent the rotor bolts from working loose. Each washer has two holes and bridges across between two adjacent bolts.

3 Apply threadlock to the bolt threads and tighten the rotor bolts to 4Nm. They usually need a six-sided Torx driver. Tighten each bolt a quarter-turn at a time, moving on to the opposite bolt and working around until they're all done up so as not to distort the rotor.

4 Once the rotor is in place you can 'set' the washers by bending them to sit flat with the head of the rotor bolt, which is three-sided. This is an added precaution that prevents the bolts from vibrating loose. Once the disc is installed, leave it for a few hours before you ride to give the Threadlock a chance to set properly.

CENTERLOCK ROTORS

1 Shimano's Centerlock mounting system uses a splined carrier on the end of the hub onto which the special rotor slides. It's a simple system that's easier to use than the six-bolt setup.

2 Apply a little anti-seize grease to the splines, being careful not to get any on the rotor itself. Carefully slide the new rotor onto the hub splines and push it home.

TOOLS REQUIRED

- **Lockring tool**
- **Adjustable spanner**
- **Anti-seize grease**

3 Put a little more anti-seize on the threads of the lockring and screw it into the end of the hub. Do it up finger-tight. If it won't tighten, make sure the threads are clean and undamaged.

4 Using a lockring tool (the splines are the same as a cassette lockring), tighten the lockring securely. It's best to use a torque wrench — 40Nm is the number to aim for.

5 Hubs with 20mm through-axles use the same rotor but a different lockring. The standard lockring is too small for a 20mm axle to pass through, so a larger lockring is used.

6 The bigger lockring is tightened using the same C-spanner as you'd use for outboard bottom bracket bearings. Tighten it securely.

USING CENTERLOCK ADAPTERS

1 It's possible to mount most six-bolt rotors to Centerlock hubs using adapters. If the rotor is one flat piece the adapters should work. Rotors with alloy spiders like some Avid, Hope and Magura units, are less likely to work.

2 Various adapters are available – this is a Shimano one, but they mostly operate on the same principles. Engage the pegs of the adapter with the bolt holes in the rotor.

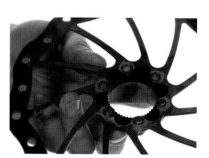

TOOLS REQUIRED

- **Circlip pliers**
- **Cassette lockring tool**
- **Large spanner**

3 Turn the rotor over and add the thin spacer, aligning the holes in the spacer with the pegs. The spacer should drop on easily, exposing the grooves in the pegs.

4 Using circlip pliers, fit the snap ring around the outside of the pegs and engage it in the grooves. This holds the adapter in place while it's not on the hub.

5 Slide the rotor and adapter assembly onto the hub as per a normal Centerlock rotor and tighten the lockring in the same way.

6 The lockring should sit inside the notched top corners of the pegs to secure the rotor. There should be no play in the rotor.

CHOOSING BRAKE ROTORS

There are many aftermarket rotors available, although the safe bet is to stick with ones from the same manufacturer as your brakes. This will ensure that the braking surface is the right size and thickness to work optimally, although as long as the rotor is the right diameter (and the braking surface deep enough) you shouldn't have any problems mixing and matching. The most common rotor sizes are 160 and 180mm, with 203mm and 140mm also available.

Bigger rotors give more stopping power and also dissipate heat better, so if you're heavy or ride fast on steep trails consider going up a size. Most brakes can be fitted with adapters to work with larger rotors. If you're not as demanding on your brakes you may be able to get away with smaller, lighter rotors. Most rotors have a simple circular edge, but some have a wavy profile. This sweeps across the pads as the rotor spins, which is supposed to reduce pad scoring and glazing. You may not notice the difference, but there's no harm in trying.

BRAKE MOUNT FACING

Post-mounts are highly tolerant of misalignment, but ISO mounts can be troublesome. They're not always well aligned out of the factory, and if the mount isn't parallel with the wheel you'll struggle to align the brake. This can be rectified using a special brake mount facing tool that removes some material from wonky mounts to give a perfectly straight, well-aligned face. These are expensive, specialist tools that you'll rarely need, so it's a job best left to a bike shop.

FITTING AND ALIGNING DISC BRAKE CALLIPERS

Fitting new disc callipers does take time to get right, although it's got easier. For a long time the ISO mount, with two bolts running sideways, was the standard, relying on fiddly shims to get the alignment right. Most brakes now are post mount, with bolts running fore and aft and slotted holes in the callipers. The callipers will either be mounted directly to the frame and fork, or there'll be an extra adapter between them. This is very common on rear brakes – ISO mounts are still common on frames, with an adapter allowing the use of a post-mount calliper. Different sized adapters are available to accommodate different rotor sizes.

1 Secure the brake calliper to the fork or frame, including the appropriate adapter. If the calliper is post mount, tighten the bolts that hold the adapter to the frame and fork first, alternating between them. Then mount the calliper to the adapter, but don't tighten the bolts fully yet. Add some Threadlock to the bolts.

TOOLS REQUIRED

• **5mm Allen key**

2 The callipers must be centred over the rotor, rather than over the pads themselves, to make sure that the pads wear evenly and to prevent vibration and any nasty noises. Make sure that the wheel is tight in the frame – if it isn't, it can slightly affect the final rotor and calliper positions.

3 Post-mount brakes are very easy to align. The calliper is mounted on slotted bolt-holes, which allow a fair bit of side-to-side movement. With the bolts slightly loosened and the wheel in the fork or frame, pull the brake on. The calliper will centre itself on the rotor – tighten the bolts to secure, then release the brake.

---

4 ISO brakes are fiddlier. Tighten both bolts then check the alignment visually. If it's off to one side, add shims (available in a range of thicknesses down to 0.2mm) between the mount and calliper – the mount is usually a little further out than it needs to be. Retighten the bolts and check again. It usually takes a few iterations to get it right.

5 Once you're happy that the rotor is centred in the calliper, tighten the fixing bolts. As a general guide, the setting will usually be 6Nm, which is not as tight as you'd expect. Take great care not to overtighten them, especially on post-mount frames or forks – stripping the threads in the frame or fork is bad news.

BLEEDING HYDRAULIC DISC BRAKES

Hydraulic disc brakes terrify most home mechanics, but the truth is they are possibly the easiest thing to set up and service. They have the advantage over cable brakes in that once they are set up properly, they need little effort to retain consistent and predictable braking. Hydraulic hoses aren't affected by dirt as cables can be and require little maintenance beyond changing pads.

You will sometimes need to 'bleed' the brake system, though. If your brakes use DOT fluid (including Avid, Hayes and Hope) regular fluid changes are recommended – DOT fluid absorbs moisture from the atmosphere, affecting performance when the fluid heats up. Mineral oil (as used by Shimano and Magura) isn't affected in the same way and is considerably less nasty to work with. Regardless of fluid, occasionally air will find its way into the system – sometimes it's there from the factory. Air bubbles give a mushy lever feel and loss of power and control, but a bleed will get rid of them.

SAFETY

Setting up hydraulic disc brakes, bleeding the system and changing hoses can be messy, so make sure you do this in a suitable environment and put something on the floor to soak up spillage. Wear an apron and some silicone rubber gloves, as brake fluid is not kind to your skin, especially DOT fluid which is corrosive.

TOOLS REQUIRED

- **Brake fluid (either mineral oil or DOT fluid – the correct one is usually marked on the brake)**
- **7 or 8mm ring spanner**
- **Bleed kit with syringe, catch bottle and tubing (these are all broadly similar but it's best to get the one recommended for your particular brakes)**

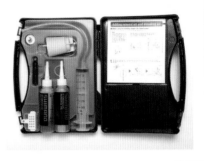

1 Air tends to rise to the top of the system, so brakes are bled from the caliper upwards, forcing air and fluid out of the lever end. Start by positioning the brake levers horizontally by loosening the clamp bolts and tilting the levers upwards.

2 Your bleed kit will have some form of catch bottle. This is a Shimano kit with a bottle that threads into a

bleed port on the lever – remove the bleed port bolt and insert the bottle. Some kits require you to take the cover off the reservoir and use a special clamp and hose to a separate bottle.

3 Brake fluid isn't good for brake pads, so it's best to take them out and put them out of harm's way. You need something in the caliper to hold the pistons apart, though, so that you can check lever action. Bleed kits usually contain a nylon block for this purpose.

▶

4 Fill the syringe from the bleed kit with fluid. Place the hose of the full syringe over the bleed nipple on the caliper, then open the valve with a spanner. Slowly push the oil into the system. You should see excess fluid – and probably air bubbles – emerging into the catch bottle.

6 Give the caliper and lever body some gentle taps with the handle of a screwdriver or similar, and waggle the hose between the two. This can sometimes dislodge air bubbles trapped in unlikely corners.

8 The Shimano bleed kit has a plunger to pop into the catch bottle so you can remove it without dumping fluid over the floor. If you're using a clamp-on bleed kit carefully remove it.

5 When there aren't any more bubbles, tighten the bleed nipple on the caliper. Pull the brake lever, which will probably allow more air to escape. Give it a three or four pulls to get it all out, then reopen the bleed nipple and push more fluid through.

7 Now check the 'bite' of the brake – that is, where the pads hit the rotor. It should feel positive and smooth without any give at the levers. If it still feels mushy, pump the lever several times and repeat step 3 to make sure the air is out of the system.

9 Replace the bleed port screw (or, if using a clamp, make sure the reservoir is topped up and then replace the diaphragm and cover). Clean excess fluid off the bars. Dispose of any used fluid properly – ask your local bike shop where they take theirs, or call the local waste authority. Do not pour brake fluid, or any non-water-soluble oils, down the drain.

MUSHY BRAKES QUICK FIX

If you have a soft brake due to air in the system, you may be able to improve matters without bleeding. Flatten the reservoir and open the cap. Fix the brake in the full-on position by pulling the lever towards the grip with a zip tie or toestrap and leave for 20–30 minutes. All the bubbles will slowly rise from inside the system. When this has finished, top up the reservoir with extra fluid (being careful not to add any bubbles) and replace the cover. The result will be sharp lever action and no mushy feel, without having to re-bleed.

REMOVING AND REPLACING HOSES

All hydraulic hoses follow the same replacement principles. Like bleeding, it's pretty simple to do. However, there are a few different types depending on which system you are using. Braided hoses, available from Goodridge and other manufacturers, are the best available. They use braided cables, which are more expensive than normal cables but give you better braking performance and a less spongy feel at the lever.

Some cable systems have factory-fitted collars, which cannot be cut. You will therefore have to specify the length of cable you need for your bike. With these systems, unlike cable-activated brakes, the amount of cable is less important to the feel at the lever. However, really long plastic cable runs do tend to flex slightly under heavy braking.

Each hose kit (enough for one brake) consists of two banjos, fixing bolts, collars, a length of hose and some O-rings. Check the manufacturer's instructions for recommended tightening torques and correct cable types before you start. Also, read through the section on bleeding (pages 91-92) as you will need to do this after the cable has been installed. Remove any brake pads and make sure that the pistons inside the callipers are flush with the inside of the calliper body. Insert a spacer into the cavity to prevent the pistons from moving.

Be careful when you remove the old hose not to splash brake fluid

TOOLS REQUIRED

- **8mm spanner**
- **Sharp knife**
- **Sharp cable cutters (shearing type)**
- **Hacksaw (sharp)**
- **Bradawl**
- **Bleeding kit**
- **A sponge and some kitchen roll**
- **Goggles and gloves**

and, although there won't be much fluid in the system, make sure you catch any waste. Wear some gloves and safety goggles as the fluid is not too kind to your skin.

Lastly, always check the cable for leaks before you ride. Tighten all the fittings and squeeze the levers hard. Leave the bike overnight and check for leaks the following day.

1 Cut braided hoses with a set of sharp cable shears. You can also use a hacksaw with a sharp blade. Measure the new cable against the old one, or cut the cable after you have installed one end securely. Always double-check the length before you cut.

2 Cut back the plastic covering 11mm down the hose. This will allow the outer collar to fit snugly over the braided part of the cable.

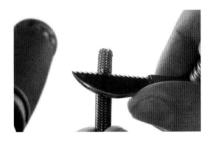

3 With a clean bradawl or 'podger', make sure that the internal PTFE (Teflon) liner is open enough to allow you to start inserting the spigot part at the end of the banjo.

4 The exposed braid will now fit into the collar. Be careful as you start to feed the cable into the collar not to fray the braid or trap it over the edge of the collar.

5 Push the collar down the cable, leaving a little gap so that the collar can rotate freely and thread easily onto the banjo spigot. The spigot has a tapered end to make insertion to the PTFE liner easier.

6 As the banjo reaches the threaded part of the collar, start to turn the collar to thread it onto the banjo. As the banjo travels further down the cable you will need more force to turn it. If you have to use pliers, cover them with duct tape or electrical tape to prevent them damaging the banjo.

7 Continue to thread the banjo into the cable, retightening the collar as necessary until it has butted up to the end of the plastic cover. When the banjo has butted up to the end of the collar, lock off the collar against it.

8 There are two O-rings per banjo that seal the system. The fixing bolt has a hole drilled down the centre and through the middle, which allows fluid to pass into the cable from either the calliper or the lever reservoir. The cable needs to be attached carefully to the calliper or brake lever and make sure no dirt or debris gets trapped in the system.

9 On XTR levers there are two prongs that locate on either side of the banjo collar. You may have to adjust the collar slightly so that the banjo can sit flat and square through these prongs and onto the lever.

10 Set the angle of the cable before you fix the other end at the lever. Make sure that there is as smooth a line as possible, to ensure that the cable doesn't kink at the collar.

11 When fitting the banjo assembly with a straight-fitting lever, fit the non-banjo type fitting first. This makes it easier to align the banjo at the calliper to the correct angle with the final turn of the spanner.

12 Lastly, once the angles have been set on the banjos and the cables are the right length, tighten up the collars and the banjo fixing bolts. You can then bleed the system to recharge it with brake fluid.

CABLE-ACTIVATED DISC BRAKES

As hydraulic brakes have become cheaper, so cable-activated disc brakes have become rarer. They're still found on entry-level mountain bikes, although they're having something of a renaissance thanks to the trend for disc brakes on cyclocross and road bikes – the integrated shifter/ brake levers on road bikes will only work with cable brakes.

Although less popular now, cable discs are still a viable option. You still get strong, consistent braking that's less affected by mud and water than rim brakes. Servicing can be done with existing tools and doesn't rely on potentially messy or hazardous brake fluid. On long tours or adventure rides, the simplicity of cables is a boon. The downside of cable discs is that they're subject to cable contamination just like conventional brakes. As the cable is an integral part of the brake, you need to follow the same rules for cable management and care as you would for V-brakes (see page 101). Looking after your cables and replacing them regularly will keep your brakes feeling as good as new.

All cable disc brakes work on a similar principle: the cable pulls a lever that activates a helical plunger which presses the pad onto the disc. Most systems rely on the rotor flexing slightly to contact the opposite pad, which is fixed in the calliper but can be adjusted for wear.

TOOLS REQUIRED

- **Torque (star-shaped) key**
- **Torque wrench**
- **Threadlock (refer to manufacturer's recommendations)**
- **Long (needle-nose) pliers**
- **Cable pullers (optional)**

1 Mount and align the calliper as for hydraulic units (see page 90). The only difference is that cable systems with one fixed pad work best with the calliper aligned such that there's a bigger gap between the rotor and the inner (fixed) pad than between the rotor and the outer (moving) pad, as measured with the pad adjusters wound right out.

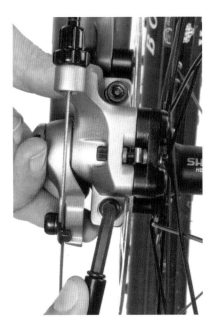

2 Pull the cable through the calliper with either a pair of pliers or a cable puller. This ensures that the cable is in the correct position and that the slack is out of the lever. Make sure that all cable housing is fully seated in the cable stops on the frame and levers.

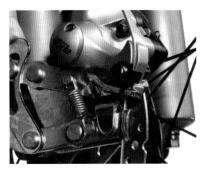

3 Tighten the Allen key bolt on the brake calliper to 7Nm. Although this bolt needs to be tight enough to prevent the cable from slipping through the clamp – if it is too tight it can crush and damage the cable, causing it to fray around the clamp. Once the cable is attached, you can stretch the cables and double-check the cable tension.

4 To bed the cables in and stretch the system, pull hard on the brake lever several times. This will also check you have done the bolts up tightly enough. Repeat steps 2 and 3 if the cable has slipped at all, or if there is excessive movement in the lever.

5 The throw of the disc calliper can be fine-tuned using the adjustment screw on the back of the calliper unit. Avid has a red button to twist for this adjustment. A good starting point for the fixed pad is to wind the adjuster in until the rotor just starts to rub with the brakes off, then back it out a couple of clicks. You'll need to readjust as the pads wear.

6 Check all the torque settings on the rotor bolts and callipers and test the brakes before you ride. Bed the pads in so that they don't glaze up. Cut the cables to length and fit end caps to prevent fraying. Keep the ends of the cables short so there's no danger of them getting caught in the brake.

QUICK-RELEASE LEVERS

Disc brakes put loads on wheel axles that rim brakes don't, which makes secure wheel attachment essential. Depending on the geometry of the brake mount and dropout, braking can cause movement of the axle in the dropout. Make sure that you use a good quality quick-release lever, preferably made of steel – Shimano quick releases are particularly good. Then tighten the lever firmly and check it regularly. Many bikes now come with through-axle systems that don't rely on an open-ended dropout – these are more secure as well as stiffer. See pages 118-122 for more on removing wheels, quick-releases and through-axles.

V-BRAKES

The V-brake is the most powerful cable-activated rim-brake design. While more straightforward to set up than cantilever brakes, care is still needed when adjusting them.

Servicing your V-brakes on a regular basis is essential – they have to be looked after carefully if you want to get the best performance from them. Regularly removing the brakes from the bike and thoroughly cleaning all the parts (using an old toothbrush to clean the mechanism) will keep them smooth. Lubricate all the pivots with a dry lube, taking care not to contaminate the pads, and make sure there is no rust on the steel parts. V-brakes are particularly sensitive to water and can seize up if neglected for long periods. So, as with most components on a mountain bike, they need to be prepared properly.

OPENING V-BRAKES

1 Unhooking the V-brakes will allow you to remove the wheels. The brake arms will swing outwards to allow the pads to clear the tyres. The secret is to squeeze the two brake arms firmly together so that the pads touch the rims. This can often be enough to slacken the cable and allow the noodle to fall out.

TOOLS REQUIRED

- **Emery cloth**
- **Grease**
- **5mm Allen key**
- **Needle-nose pliers**
- **Torque wrench**

2 With your free hand grab the noodle and pull it sideways and away from the opposite calliper. This will pop the head of the noodle out of the retaining cage. Pull the cable through the slot in this cage. Don't wrench the cable out as it can damage the cable inner – you do need to be firm but don't jerk at the noodle.

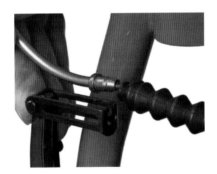

3 When replacing the noodle, it is essential to make sure that the noodle head is placed securely into the retaining cage. It is possible for the noodle to snag on the edge of this cage and give the impression that it is inserted correctly, so always double check. Lastly, pull hard on the lever to check the action is perfect.

4 This is what the V-brake should look like when reassembled. If you are still having trouble releasing the brakes, you can use the brake adjuster on the lever to give a little more slack, or undo the bolt on the calliper itself and let a little cable through.

FITTING V-BRAKES

1 Prepare the cantilever studs (otherwise known as brake bosses) on the frame. If they are rusty, or if the brakes are a little rough and notchy in their action, you may need to clean off the stud with some emery cloth. Use a thin strip of a fine grade so that the finish is smooth.

2 Grease the faces of the cantilever stud, as it often acts as a pivot for the brake. Some better quality brakes have their own bearing inside the brake arm. Some brakes have a brass sleeve that fits snugly over the canti stud – this is the bush that the brake pivots on. Greasing this and checking it regularly will also prevent the stud from rusting up and the brake sticking or seizing onto the bike.

3 The base of the stud may have three small holes on it – the one pictured just has one. These holes retain the stopper pin on the back of the brake, securing the brake and enabling the spring to act against the brake lever to return the brake to the open position. On cantilever brakes you can choose a hole to adjust the strength of the return springs. V-brake springs should be fitted into the central holes.

4 Insert the fixing bolts. They come coated with a locking compound that prevents them vibrating loose under braking forces. A little thin oil or light smear of anti-seize compound will prevent the threads from rusting up.

5 Tighten the fixing bolts to around 7Nm using a torque wrench. This will need to be re-checked once in a while as vibrations can shake the bolts loose. Make sure there's no significant slop in the brakes on the studs.

6 The pads are curved to follow the shape of the rim. Make sure that the pads are set just below the top of the rim (about 2mm), but the pads should also be flat in order to act upon all the braking surface of the rim. Also check that the pads are facing in the right direction and are on the correct calliper arm (usually marked left and right on the brake pad).

ADJUSTING V-BRAKE PADS

Some V-brakes have parallelogram mechanisms that keep the pads perpendicular to the rim at all times for consistent braking and even pad wear. It's still important to get the pad alignment just right, though. The procedure is the same for simpler V-brakes without linkages.

1 The pad is fully adjustable for angle as the retaining washers and spacers act as a ball joint, which allows the pad to be moved to hit the rim from any angle. Make sure that the wheel is centred in the bike before you start to adjust the pad angle as this can make a big difference.

2 First of all, loosely fit the pads to the rim so you can have a look at the setup. The distance between the noodle-retaining cage and the fastening bolt should be over 39mm with the pads on the rim. This distance will be influenced by the rim width and the position of the canti studs. You can tweak it by swapping around the concave washers (which are different thicknesses) to move the arms away from the rim.

3 The best way to adjust the pad angle is to hold the pad in place with one hand and the Allen key in the other. Make small adjustments and always keep the pads symmetrical. If the pads are hard to adjust or will not stay in place, check that the domed washers are installed correctly. Once the pads are set, hold them in place while tightening the nuts to 9–10Nm.

4 There is some 'toe-in' set on these pads, which allows the pad to be 'sucked in' towards the rim as the brake is applied. Set the cables so that there is a gap of about 1–2mm on either side of the rim. In this position the toe-in should be no more than 1mm from front to back.

5 Once you are happy that the pads are tight and set at the correct angle and height you can centre the brake properly. This will affect how the brake feels at the lever, so check that is still feels easy to apply the brakes. Give the brake a few hard pulls to check that it returns and that the wheel can spin without rubbing.

REPLACING CARTRIDGE-TYPE PADS

The best type of pad is one that allows you to replace the rubber part only and has an aluminium backing that stays in place. This 'cartridge' system only needs setting up once and you can change pads quickly.

1 Pull out the split pin from the top of the shoe (you may need to push it up from the bottom and catch hold of it with a pair of needle-nose pliers). It is likely that the pin will be bent or dropped on the floor, so it's best to replace the pin too. All good-quality replacement pads will come with a pair of spare pins.

2 Slide the old pad out of the shoe and the new one in. Make sure you are using the correct pad (they are usually marked left and right). If you are in doubt, look for the channel in the back of the pad where the split pin slots through and secures it to the shoe. Replace the pin.

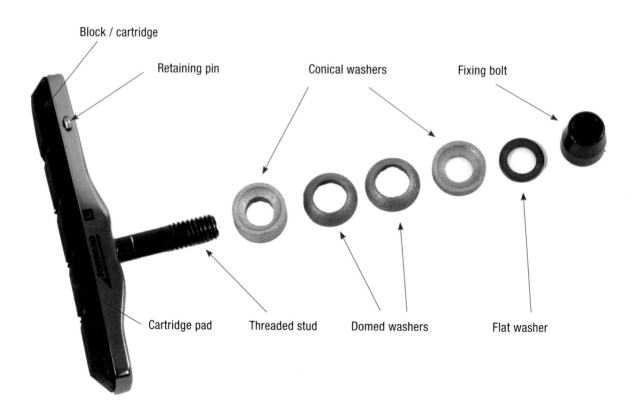

Block / cartridge

Retaining pin

Conical washers

Fixing bolt

Cartridge pad

Threaded stud

Domed washers

Flat washer

V-BRAKE CABLE REPLACEMENT

You should check for cable trouble on a regular basis and always take care of your cables when releasing the brakes to remove the wheels, as they are vulnerable and susceptible to kinking. Kinked cables and water inside the outers will hinder your braking considerably. It's hard to tell when the inner wire is kinked but a sloppy or stiff feeling in the lever action is a dead give-away. Replacing the cable run is the best way to solve this, but stripping out the inner and using a quality spray lube can be a short-term fix.

It's pretty rare for a brake cable to fray dangerously, but it's worth checking the inner cable, especially if the brakes are feeling stiffer than usual. This friction can be caused by the inner cable rubbing on either a burr on the outer cable or a frame cable stop. It's also rare for cables to snap, but they can fray at the clamp bolts which can make future adjustment difficult.

You can adjust cable tension at the levers 'on the fly' using the adjusters on the lever at the handlebar. Simply unscrew the centre section and the inner cable will tighten. Then lock it off with the outer lock ring. Check the lever a few times and make sure you have left enough play for the wheel to spin freely. We ran through lever reach in 'Before you ride' on page 34. However, adjusting the reach can affect the pull of the brake lever, so long-term adjustment of the slack in

TOOLS REQUIRED

- **5mm Allen key**
- **Cable cutters**
- **Pliers**
- **Grease**

a cable system is best done by pulling the cable through at the brake-cable fastening bolt on the calliper.

1 Cables can be removed from the levers by turning the barrel adjuster so that the slot lines up with the slot in the brake lever body. Release the brakes at the callipers and then pull gently on the lever. As you release the lever, the cable will slacken and the inner cable can be fed through this slot.

2 The nipple can then be unhooked from the lever. Be careful when you return the cables and make sure that the cables are properly relocated into the adjusters, noodles and frame stops, so that they cannot slip out when the brake is applied.

3 Mountain bike brake cables have a barrel nipple that rotates slightly in the lever every time you pull on the brakes. Greasing the nipple will prevent friction and stop any noises developing as the levers are applied. Inspect the nipples regularly and check for any signs of wear and tear on the cable.

4 The cable 'noodle' pipe comes in two lengths. Assuming you have the front brake lever on the right, you'll need the longer 170 degree one on the front brake and the shorter 90 degree one on the rear. Depending on how the brake cable routes along the frame, the 170 degree may work better on the rear too – choose whichever gives the smoothest cable run.

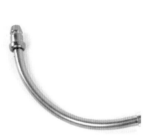

5 The 'noodle' has a nylon insert that provides protection for the cable and also helps prevent friction in this part of the cable run. When new these pipes have a small amount of grease squirted into them and it's a good idea to check regularly that the cable is still well lubricated. Use a very small amount of waterproof grease and inject it with a grease gun.

6 Cable outers should be measured (it's easiest to use the old cables as a template) and cut using a quality cable cutter. Make sure that the ends of the cable are flat – they can be tidied up with a metal file – and that the inner nylon part is open at the ends.

7 Unlike gear cables, it's only necessary to add a ferrule to the cable outer where the cable will contact the frame stops. The V-brake noodle has its own built-in ferrule. New brake cables usually have a factory fitted ferrule on one end. Start with this one at the lever adjuster.

8 The rear brake cable must be accurately cut so that the curve of the cable is unhindered and smooth. Over-long cables flap about, create excess friction and can also catch passing undergrowth. However, short cables will pull on the callipers when steering and potentially de-centralise them over the rims.

9 Cable doughnuts are used to prevent the cable slapping on the top tube and wearing out the paintwork. The noise of flapping cables is also highly annoying. It's possible to use plastic sleeves instead, although these can retain moisture which will eventually corrode the cables.

10 The rubber gaiter covers the cable as it exits the noodle and prevents any water and mud getting in. They are not essential and the brake will work perfectly well without them. However, the noodle is the weak link in the V-brake system and needs constant care. It's always worth re-lubricating the noodle after wet rides.

11 Thread the cable through the fixing bolt. With the lever barrel adjuster wound out a couple of turns, pull the callipers together with the cable. Fasten the inner cable into the calliper using a 5mm Allen key. Wind the barrel adjuster back in to give the necessary pad clearance. Leave a couple of inches of cable to allow for further adjustment and cut the cable with a sharp cable cutter.

12 Lastly, add a cable end cap to prevent the cable from fraying. This will prevent injury and enable you to make further adjustments to the brakes. Tuck the end of the cable out of the way – some brake arms have a nub for this purpose, or tuck it behind the spring anchor pin on the arm.

V-BRAKE TIPS

1 Ceramic rims are a great idea for V-brakes if you are having trouble stopping. They do require special pads, as standard rubber pads can wreck the surface, glazing it up and making it unusable.

2 Clean rims will make a huge difference to brake performance. Use disc-brake cleaner or a special 'rim rubber' to clean your rims and regularly remove all the grime that builds up, as brake dust will just act as an abrasive and wear down both the rim and the pads.

3 Squealing is caused by vibration. Toe in the pads and you'll alleviate the problem. However, if this still doesn't work there may be excessive play in the brake assembly and it may need to be replaced.

4 V-brake pads wear fairly evenly and slowly in the dry. However, in the wet you can wear through a set in a matter of hours, especially if it's muddy. As V-brake pads are usually very low profile, they wear out in a matter of months in the summer and weeks in the winter. If you want razor-sharp braking from V-brakes, fit some ceramic rims and ceramic-compatible pads.

5 Over-long cables will usually add friction and absorb braking power, so keep the cable lengths to a minimum without sacrificing movement in the handlebars and suspension systems. You should replace the nylon noodle insert if it is damaged, and oil and replace cables regularly.

6 Braking can be improved at the lever by adjusting the lever pull. Many brake levers have adjustable cable positions to offer more or less leverage from the lever. The more leverage you have, the sharper the brake will be. Avid levers have a special knob, which can be dialled by hand. Shimano V-brake levers have either an adjustment knob or a plastic block that can be removed. This can make the brakes sharper, so test-ride the bike before you try anything too extreme.

08

CONTACT POINTS

You and your bike meet at five points – one saddle, two pedals and two handlebar grips. These points between them have to take all your weight and transfer all your pedalling efforts to the transmission. Turns, wheelies, jumps and all other manoeuvres are initiated through the contact points. So it's essential that they're all in top condition, secure and reliable.

Fortunately this is a reasonably straightforward task, as usually only the pedals have any moving parts. For the rest, it's a case of making sure that all fasteners are adequately (but not excessively) tight and that the components themselves aren't about to fail. The consequences of broken parts aren't usually pleasant – you might manage to break a seatpost without hurting yourself, but if a handlebar goes you're almost certainly on the ground very suddenly. Keep a close eye on these critical components.

FITTING HANDLEBARS

The trend for mountain bike bars is towards more width. In the early 1990s a 580mm (23in) bar was considered wide, but that would be exceptionally narrow by today's standards. XC race bikes may still be equipped with flat 580mm bars, but for all-round trail bikes even 680mm (26.75in) is on the narrow side – plenty of bikes come with 720mm (28.4in) or wider, and it's possible to get bars over 760mm (30in) wide.

Such wide bars work well with modern bikes, which tend to have relaxed head angles and short stems. Such a setup isn't for everyone, though, especially if you're below average height or ride densely wooded trails. While it's best to buy handlebars at the length you are going to use them, that's not always practical – bars aren't usually available in a large range of widths, with manufacturers assuming that you'll cut them down to suit you. It's possible to cut down aluminium and carbon bars.

1 Before installing handlebars, ensure that the inside of the stem clamp is free from any sharp edges or burrs that may lead to stress risers in the bar and possible failure. Sharp corners at the edge of the bar clamp can be easily rectified with a small half-round needle file.

TOOLS REQUIRED

- **Hairspray**
- **An old spoke**
- **Stanley knife**
- **Pair of pincers**
- **Zip ties**
- **Griptite or touch-up paint (for permanent fixing)**
- **Set of Allen keys**

2 Almost every mountain bike stem has a detachable face plate, allowing the bars to be removed without disturbing the shifters, brake levers or grips. It's essential to tighten the faceplate bolts evenly. For the common four-bolt face plate, tighten the bolts a little at a time going from one corner to the opposite corner, then across or up, then diagonally to the final bolt. At this stage do them up just enough to stop the bar rotating.

CUTTING CARBON

While carbon fibre is reasonably easy to cut, the fine dust that results is somewhat unpleasant. While the long-term health effects of inhaling carbon fibre dust are uncertain, the likelihood of short-term irritation is well established. Cut bars or seatposts in a well-ventilated area, wear a dust mask, gloves and eye protection.

3 Even with a perfectly smooth bar clamp, take care when installing bars not to twist them in the stem too much. This can scratch the surface of the bar, which creates a stress riser and can fail at a later date. There is usually a mark or series of marks on the bar where the centre section is. This will also give you an idea of the preferred angle of the sweep. Line this up with the front cap of the stem.

4 Centre the bars in the stem. Again, there are usually guide marks on the bar to show you where this is. If in doubt, measure from each side of the bar clamp to the ends of the bars. If it needs to move, you may need to slightly loosen the clamp bolts again.

5 Most mountain bikes have riser bars, with the grip sections positioned higher than the centre. Angle the bars so that the sweep of the grip sections is up and back, roughly in line with your arms when seated. On most bars this position coincides with the centre section of the bar being in a vertical plane.

6 Position the controls at equal distances from the stem. Do not over-tighten them, as the levers are sensitive and could bend if they are not allowed to 'move' a little in the event of a crash. Usually the brake levers and shifters have their own separate clamps.

HANDLEBAR TIPS

1   Most creaking noises from handlebars can easily be eliminated by stripping the bar from the stem, cleaning it with parts cleaner (disc-brake cleaner is good for this) and rebuilding the stem with fresh grease or copper slip on the fixing bolts. Take the stem off, check the steerer for corrosion and clean it too. Take the opportunity to inspect the bars – if there are any cracks, deep gouges or mysterious discolouration, replace them.

2   Bars don't last forever. They can be damaged in crashes, and in the case of carbon fibre bars damage isn't always visible. Aluminium bars will eventually fatigue and start to crack, although this could take many years. Several manufacturers recommend replacing bars and stems every two to three years even if they haven't been crashed. The consequences of a sudden bar or stem failure are unlikely to be pleasant, so regular replacement is a good idea.

7 Sometimes the brake lever and shifter will share a clamp – this is SRAM's Matchmaker system. The controls are still independently adjustable, but there's just a single bolt securing them to the bars.

8 Finish off with final tightening of the stem clamp bolts. Then fit the grips (see page 108 for more information). Check the angle of the bar and positions of the controls, and check all the bolts for tightness before riding.

GRIPS

1 Most new bikes come with lock-on grips. These have an internal plastic sleeve that slides easily onto the handlebar and is secured in place by pinch bolts in alloy collars at one or both ends. If you don't already have lock-on grips, get some next time yours need replacing – they're much easier to work with than the traditional stuck-on grips.

2 To remove a lock-on grip, simply loosen the pinch bolts and slide the grip off. Take care with the bolts, which are usually tiny and quite easy to round out the heads of. You may have to move the shifters or brake lever to access the bolt head. Some grips combine the outer collar with an end cap, others have a push-in plastic cap. This will come off with the grip.

3 Refitting the grip is the opposite of removal. Orient the grip so that the locking bolts are accessible around the shifter and brake lever to make removing them easier next time. Retighten the bolts, being careful not to round or strip them. Replace the end caps.

4 Conventional one-piece rubber grips are a little harder to remove. Even if they're not stuck on, the friction between the grip and the bar is usually substantial. If you're not going to reuse them, you can cut them off with a Stanley knife, taking care not to scratch the bars. If you want to use them again, wiggle an old spoke under the grip and spray a bit of WD-40 into the gap. Work around the grip until it slides off.

5 Use some hairspray to fit the grips. This will allow you to push the grip on very easily, and it also sets like a lacquer and seals the grip to the bar. It's not sticky though, so it won't make a mess of your bars and so on. If you use Gripshift shifters, always use the plastic washer they provide to enable the shifter to rotate without binding to the grip.

6 If you are fitting bar ends, you'll need to push the grips on far enough to make room on the end of the bar. Make sure you don't over-tighten bar ends; they only need to be tight enough so you don't move them with riding force. It's best to let them move a bit to protect your bike in the event of a crash – if they are too tight then you risk twisting the bar as well as damaging the bar end. Always put a plug in the end of the bar – crashing with open-ended bars is very dangerous.

SEATPOSTS

1 Aluminium seatposts should have a light coating of grease before being inserted into the seat tube. Carbon fibre posts shouldn't be greased – if they won't stay put, use some carbon-specific assembly paste. The post should slide in without any pressure being applied and there shouldn't be any side-to-side movement before the clamp bolt is tightened. Seatposts need to be quickly adjustable for height – if you're riding steep downhills or drop-offs it helps to tuck the seat well out of the way – so the grease will prevent it from seizing in the frame and getting scratched.

TOOLS REQUIRED

- **Allen keys**
- **Grease or assembly paste**
- **Spirit level**

2 The seatpost is held in place by a locking collar on the frame. This will either be a quick-release lever (as shown) or a simple Allen bolt. Seat collars tend to get covered in water and grit from the rear wheel and this can prevent them from clamping effectively. If it uses a bolt, make sure that the threads and under the head are greased. A quick-release lever should have grease on the threads and between the cam and follower on the lever itself. Don't overtighten either type – just enough to stop the post spinning or slipping is adequate.

3 The saddle is secured to the seatpost by a clamp that holds the saddle rails. There are many different designs of saddle clamp – this one uses a single sideways bolt to clamp everything together, but you'll find single vertical bolts, twin bolts either side of the shaft, one bolt and one adjuster wheel and lots of other variations. Usually you can remove and fit the saddle without having to dismantle the whole clamp. Make sure all mating surfaces and bolt threads are greased.

4 Saddle position is important, so spend a bit of time getting it right. Having the saddle level is a good starting point. We're using a spirit level here, but you can also sight across the top of the saddle to something horizontal – brick walls are useful for this. Find out more about saddle positioning on page 32.

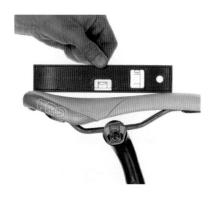

FAILURES

The worst-case scenario is a snap, but this will usually be the result of riding around on a bent post for a while and thus placing too much stress on the material; the constant bending results in a fatigue fracture. You can easily check for a bend by placing a straight edge next to it and eying it up front and back and side to side. Do this regularly, especially after a crash. The clamp can break in various places, the yokes (the two halves that clamp the saddle rails together) can snap or the serrations that hold the cradle on some designs can wear smooth and leave you with your saddle pointing skyward. Some cheap bonded clamps (where the clamp is glued and push-fitted into the shaft) are also prone to failure; this is not normally dangerous but very annoying and well worth avoiding.

CHOOSING A SEATPOST
MATERIALS

Seatposts are usually made out of aluminium. The best posts are made from butted Easton EA 70 tubing, 7075-T6 or 6061-T6. Cro-mo steel posts are strong and therefore great for dirt jumpers, but they do weigh a bit more. Steel is also better if you want to use an extra-long post (more than 300mm). Some posts have carbon fibre shafts.

LENGTH

Seatposts come in several lengths, with 350mm and 400mm being the most common. You need a post that leaves plenty of material in the frame. They usually have a line to indicate the minimum insertion level (or maximum height). This should be no higher than the top of the frame. Do not exceed this – it not only protects the seatpost, but also prevents placing excess strain on the top of the frame's seat tube/clamp area, which can easily be distorted by the extra leverage on the little bit left in the frame. Regardless of the marks on the seatpost, you should always have at least 50mm (2in) of seatpost extending below the point at which the top tube joins the seat tube.

SIZE

It's essential to get the correct size of seatpost for your frame. Fortunately this is simpler than it used to be. Modern bikes have largely standardised on 27.2, 30.9 or 31.6mm. Most steel frames are 27.2mm, most aluminium and carbon frames use one of the others, although as with all generalisations there are plenty of exceptions in both cases. Older bikes may need anything from 26.4mm upwards, and there are bikes out there that take 25mm or 34.9mm. Even 0.2mm either way can make a difference to the correct fit. If it is too big, it can be difficult to fit or remove; if it is too small, it can move about and damage the collar and distort the top of the seat tube.

DROPPER POSTS

Dropper posts are telescopic, with a steel or air spring and release mechanism inside. A lever, which may be positioned under the seat or remotely on the bars, activates the release mechanism and allows the seat to be lowered while riding for easier descending. At the bottom, another flick of the lever pops the seat back up to pedalling height. All dropper posts need periodic maintenance, but the requirements vary considerably – consult your manual for details. Remote levers will need cable maintenance in the same way as gear and brake cables – see page 101.

PEDALS

Mountain bike pedals get a lot of abuse. They stick out from the bike at the bottom of your pedal stroke and are the first thing to collide with rocks or logs at the side of the trail. Being positioned so low, they also collect more than their fair share of mud, water and grit.

While many mountain bikers used toe clips and straps on caged pedals in the early days, these are all but extinct now. For most riders, pedal choice comes down to clip-in units (also known, confusingly, as 'clipless' because they did away with toe clips) that use shoe-mounted metal cleats to lock in to a sprung retention mechanism, or flat pedals, with small pins to provide grip on a flat-soled shoe. It's a matter of personal preference – clip-in pedals are more efficient and many riders find the added security helps confidence, but just as many prefer the freedom of movement and ability to quickly bail out of flats.

Pedal maintenance varies, but a lot of pedals use a similar bearing setup to Shimano SPD units and it's these that we look at here.

FITTING PEDALS

1 The most important thing to remember about pedals is that pedals have a left- and right-hand thread. Most systems stamp 'L' and 'R' on the axle somewhere so you know which is which. This refers to the side of the bike that the pedal is supposed to go on. On Shimano pedals the stamp is usually on the flat part of the pedal spindle, where the spanner attaches.

2 Pedal threads must be greased. Use a quality waterproof synthetic or an anti-seize grease. Clean the threads and regrease them regularly. Because axles are made out of steel and cranks are made out of aluminium, there can be problems with threads. Be careful not to cross-thread the cranks as they will be ruined.

TOOLS REQUIRED

- **Waterproof synthetic or anti-seize grease**
- **Torque wrench**
- **Allen key**
- **Lubricant**
- **Pedal collar tool**
- **Vice**
- **Grease**
- **Spanners**

3 Many cranks come with washers that should be inserted between the pedal and the crank arm. These are designed to prevent fretting damage to the face of the crank from the shoulders of the pedal axle. With carbon fibre and lightweight aluminium cranks, this can lead to failure.

4 The drive-side (right-hand) pedal is a right-hand thread, tightening clockwise in the conventional manner. The non-drive-side (left-hand) pedal is a left-hand thread. This means that both sides tighten towards the front of the bike. The easiest way to remember this is to hold the pedal up to the crank, flat on your fingers, and spin the cranks backwards as if you were freewheeling.

5 Tighten the pedals to the manufacturer's recommended torque setting. Hold the opposite crank or the rear wheel and use the added leverage to help you tighten the pedals. To remove the pedals, it is probably easiest if you stand the bike on the floor. You will remove the pedal in the direction of the freewheel, so you may have to hold the opposite crank to prevent it from spinning.

6 As well as spanner flats on the axle, most pedals also have a hexagonal hole for an Allen key in the end. This can be accessed from the back of the crank arm. Some lightweight pedals can only be fitted and removed this way. Use a long Allen key and watch your hands on the chainrings.

7 If you are using SPD pedals for the first time, back the springs off so that the release tension is minimal. This will make it easier to engage and disengage. You can increase tension as your confidence builds. As the pedal is double-sided and has a spring for each side, make sure you loosen the bolts on both sides of the pedal.

8 Regular cleaning and lubrication is essential. Make sure there are no small stones lodged in the spring plates. A few drops of light oil on the pivots of the retention mechanism will keep it running smoothly. Periodically you'll need to service the pedal bearings too.

PEDAL BEARING SERVICING

There are many different kinds of pedal on the market. We're looking at Shimano SPD units here, as they're the most popular. Some other pedals can be serviced in a similar way.

1 Dry or gritty bearings can be cleaned and regreased, and loose bearings tightened. Binding bearings may suggest a bent axle. Most Shimano pedals use the same replaceable cartridge-style axle. There is a special tool to undo the collars on the pedals.

2 Place the special collar tool in a vice and loosen the pedal (there is an arrow on the pedal collar to show you which direction to turn it). The pedal body can be removed and cleaned thoroughly with degreaser and a toothbrush.

3 With the axle removed, you can assess the damage. Hold the bearing part and spin the axle stub. If it is wobbly and the bearings are very loose, you will probably have to replace the complete assembly. Slight looseness can be adjusted out.

4 Remove the lock nut and the top cone. If the bearings are dull and pitted and the cones have similar pitting and marks, you will be better off replacing the complete unit. You can adjust the cones with this special tool or with the appropriate sized spanners. It's a very fiddly job and it's very easy to lose the 3/32-inch bearings. If you are stripping the axle, you'll need fresh bearings and grease. Readjusting the cones is very similar to adjusting wheel bearings. You are looking to set the collar so it has no play and isn't binding onto the bearings.

5 Before replacing a new axle or the restored old one, pack the pedal body with grease. Don't fill the pedal body right to the top, there needs to be space for the axle to fit back in. Ideally you need slightly more grease than will fit, so a small amount of fresh grease purges the inner bearing as you tighten the axle unit.

6 Tighten the pedal body onto the axle using the same tool. You only need to tighten it by hand – over-tightening can break the collar and bind the bearings. The pressure of the grease being forced through the bearing can make it hard to turn – if you're really struggling, take out some of the grease from the pedal body and try again.

SPD PEDAL CLEATS

SPD and other clipless pedals use a metal cleat bolted to the sole of the shoe to click into the pedal. You need the appropriate shoes, but all mountain bike pedal systems use the same two-bolt fitting. Most shoes come ready to fit the cleats, although some will have a rubber cover over the cleat nuts. This may be held in place by bolts through the nuts, or you may have to cut the cover out with a Stanley knife.

Regular cleaning and lubrication is essential for reliable and consistent performance. In particular, stones, grit or dried mud around the cleat can prevent it from clicking into the pedal. Pick out any such obstructions. Lubricate the cleats regularly to prevent them from rusting up, as rust will wear the pedal and cleat out more quickly.

TOOLS REQUIRED

- **Anti-seize grease**
- **Pen**
- **Torque wrench**
- **4mm Allen bit**
- **Duct tape**

1 Prepare the threads in the plates with an anti-seize grease. The bolts will rust pretty quickly and become impossible to remove if you don't. You can replace these screws with stainless steel bolts (you can buy these from an engineering supplier) as they are less likely to rust up and will therefore last longer.

2 Some shoes don't have a built-in threaded plate but require one to be added from the inside. Lift up the part of the insole behind the cleat box and push the plate in so that it fits into the slots in the sole.

3 Assess the position of the ball of your foot over the pedal axle. Mark on the side of your shoe where the ball of your foot is, then mark a line across the sole of your shoe. Use this reference to decide which set of holes in the plates to use. Check the angle that your feet naturally rest at by sitting on a high stool with your feet dangling. Angle the cleats accordingly.

4 The correct cleat position is with the ball or pushing part of your foot over the pedal axle. This requires measuring and some trial and error to get spot-on. It's also best to get someone to help you do this job, as you can only adjust the cleat position properly once the cleats are in place.

5 When you're happy with the position of the cleats, tighten the bolts to the recommended torque setting. Alternate between the two bolts, tightening a little at a time. Do not over-tighten them as the threads can strip very easily, in which case you would have to replace the sole insert.

6 Shoes usually come with a sticker to cover the slots in the sole on the inside, both to prevent the shoe plate rubbing on the insole and to stop water coming in. If you don't have the sticker, duct tape works equally well.

REMOVING WORN CLEATS

If you applied plenty of anti-seize when you fitted the cleats, they shouldn't be too hard to remove. The main difficulty is that the bolt heads tend to get deformed by walking on rocks, making it hard to engage an Allen key sufficiently to undo them. Often simply tapping the Allen key in with a hammer is enough to get it past the burrs in the head. Make sure it's well engaged or the head will round out. If all else fails, you'll have to drill the bolt heads out. This is time-consuming as the bolts are very hard. Use progressively larger drill bits until the head pops off. You should then be able to extract the rest of the bolt with pliers.

PEDAL TIPS

- Noisy or creaking pedals can be due to worn cleats or simply dry threads. Regrease the threads regularly and replace your cleats before they start to release on their own. It's not only annoying, it can also be dangerous.

- The cleat on the side you release most often when you stop will wear more quickly than the other one, so swap them around for a longer life.

09

WHEELS

We tend to take wheels for granted. It's easy to forget what remarkable things they are. Bicycle wheels are one of the most efficient structures around, deriving enormous strength from lightweight parts. The secret is the spoke tension. Bike wheels are pre-stressed structures. Loads applied to the wheel from rocks, roots, landings, crashes or just riding along tend to make part of the wheel get a bit looser, but if the starting tension is high enough nothing ever actually gets loose – it just gets a bit less tight. By distributing the loads across all the spokes, wheels manage their amazing feats of strength.

They can't be left to it, though. It's important to check and, if necessary, maintain that all-important tension. The moving parts of wheels need attention too. Hub bearings take a lot of stick, what with having to support the whole weight of the bike and rider while being quite near the ground and subject to attack from water, mud, grit, dust and all sorts of other hostile substances.

REMOVING WHEELS

Nearly every mountain bike has quick-release wheels, although the traditional system of open-ended dropouts and a quick-release skewer through the axles is gradually being replaced by through-axle setups where the whole axle slides out. Through-axles guarantee wheel alignment, hold wheels more securely and provide a stiffer connection between wheel and frame. They're not as fast to use as the traditional QR, though, which is still dominant on race-oriented bikes.

Both systems are useful for repairing punctures or putting your bike into the back of your car. But both can be potentially hazardous if done up incorrectly. On most mountain bikes the front-wheel system has a slightly different technique from the rear-wheel system. If you are removing both wheels, take the front one out first; this will make the bike easier to manage and means that you won't have to drag the chain and gears on the ground.

Most modern mountain bikes have disc brakes from which wheels will just drop out. If you have a bike with V-brakes you'll need to unhook the brake cable first to allow clearance for the tyres to pass through.

SAFETY

Tightening the QR adequately is essential for safety if you have disc brakes, especially on the front wheel. Disc brakes put more loads onto the axle and in extreme cases can make the wheel shift in the dropouts if the quick release is a poor design or installed incorrectly. Check your QRs regularly, especially before riding.

Also, be careful where you position the lever in the closed position. If it faces forwards or down, it can catch on undergrowth and come undone. Different frame and fork designs accommodate different lever positions, but the front one pointing upwards parallel and close to the fork leg works with most.

With most bikes now equipped with disc brakes, it's important to remember that discs get hot. If you get a puncture on a fast downhill, the brake rotor could well be hot enough to burn you. Keep your fingers clear of the rotor when removing the wheels and keep your gloves on.

FRONT WHEELS – QUICK RELEASE

1 Safety tabs are designed to prevent the wheel from falling out should the quick-release (QR) lever be done up too loosely. They are also known as 'lawyer lips' because of several well-publicised US lawsuits in the early days of the mountain bike. A few companies were sued over front wheels dropping out of the forks unannounced, which had catastrophic results. This was usually to do with poor installation than mechanical failure and is also the reason for the big disclaimer sticker on the bike telling you to do up your QRs before your first ride.

2 Because of the tabs, you'll need to both open the QR lever and undo the nut on the opposite side a little to allow the wheel to come out. Two or three turns is usually enough. The key here is to remember how much you have undone it and not to remove it completely. The wheel will then drop out.

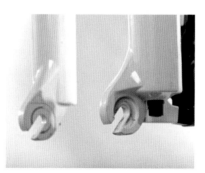

3 The springs on the inside of the quick-release mechanism help centralise the nut and the lever to push them away from the bike. They also make it easier to replace the wheel, as you don't have to centre the assembly. This leaves your hands free to hold the bike and the wheel.

4 The front wheel has to be firmly placed into the dropouts before you can do up the lever. Replace the wheels with the bike on the ground. This way the weight of the bike can help make the wheels go in straight.

FRONT WHEELS – THROUGH-AXLE

1 Through-axle systems like the Maxle or QR15 don't have a separate QR skewer. Instead the whole axle comes out. They have a familiar-looking lever on one end, which is the first thing to open. Maxles have the lever on the right, QR15 on the left.

2 Both through-axle systems feature holes in the fork legs rather than open-ended dropouts. This means that the wheel can't fall out, although it could work loose – if you feel any looseness or rattling from the front end, stop and check.

ADJUSTING QUICK-RELEASE SKEWERS

Once the wheel is slotted into the dropouts, slowly tighten the nut up until the lever starts to tighten. When the lever is directly in line with the skewer, as shown here, that is enough – this will ensure that the lever will close tightly enough. It should take a firm push to close – if it leaves a mark on a bare hand, it's sufficiently tight. If it's too easy to close, it's too easy to open too.

3 With the lever open, you can use it as a handle to unscrew the axle from the threads in the fork. Maxles require the open lever to be engaged in the slot on the end of the axle to unscrew them.

4 Once the axle is disengaged from the threads it will pull straight out. Sometimes they stick in the hub – Maxles stick out on the non-lever side and can be tapped across; if a QR15 axle needs help you'll need a suitable tool to insert into the threaded end before tapping.

5 With the axle out, the wheel will drop out of the forks. The ends of the hub engage in pockets on the inside of the fork legs to ensure good alignment. It can be quite a snug fit between the fork legs – you may have to wiggle it a bit before it comes out.

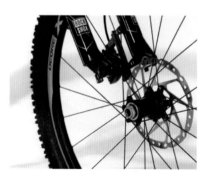

6 To put the wheel back in, align the brake rotor with the calliper and push the wheel back into the pockets. Reinsert the axle. You need to screw it in until it stops, then tighten the lever. Maxle levers can be tightened to point in any direction. The closing tension can be adjusted using the nut on the opposite end.

7 QR15 levers have to close in the direction they're pointing when tight. This should be either towards the back of the bike or vertically alongside the fork leg. If it's in the wrong place, take it out and remove the small bolt in the threaded insert on the right-hand fork leg.

8 With the bolt removed, the insert can be popped out and reinserted at a different orientation. Use the numbers for reference. The axle will now become tight in a position that lets the lever close in a useful direction.

REAR WHEELS – QUICK RELEASE

1 The chain should be on the smallest sprocket at the back and the largest chainring, so make sure you change into this gear before you start. This makes it easier to get the chain off the cassette and easier to replace the wheel afterwards.

2 Stand behind the bike and hold the bike upright with your legs trapping the wheel, leaving your hands free to remove the wheel. Now undo the lever. Rear dropouts don't have safety tabs because the chain helps to keep the wheel in, so there's no need to undo the nut.

3 The wheel will remain trapped into the bike by the chain, so twist the derailleur backwards to release the wheel. The chain should stay on the front chainwheel, so it will be easier if you start with the chain in this position when you replace the wheel.

4 To replace the rear wheel, the derailleur needs to spring into the correct position with the wheel in the bike. Next, wrap the chain over the top of the smallest sprocket to help the wheel slot into the dropouts. Take care to line the disc brake up centrally to the pads in the calliper.

5 Pull the wheel upwards and backwards, and it should slot into place easily. If it doesn't, the wheel may have become snagged on the brake pads or the derailleur may not be in the correct gear position.

6 Do not adjust the nut on the QR lever as the rear wheel should clear the dropouts and slip in easily. However, it is worth checking that the lever feels tight as it closes. Rest your weight on the bike as this will keep the wheel central in the rear dropouts.

REAR WHEELS – THROUGH AXLE

1 Through-axle systems are increasingly common on rear wheels, with the most common being a 12mm axle at a hub 142mm wide. There's a version of the Maxle in this size, which works in the same way as the front Maxle. Or you may find an X12 axle, which unscrews from the left-hand side using a 5mm Allen key.

2 With the axle removed, the wheel comes out in the same way as with a conventional quick release. Pull the derailleur backwards to get the chain and jockey wheels out of the way.

3 Replacing the wheel is the reverse process. As with front through axles, rear systems rely on the ends of the hub engaging in pockets on the frame. You'll need to get the brake rotor lined up with the calliper before the wheel will go fully home.

4 It can take a few tries to get everything lined up on both sides. As with front wheels, it's easiest to do this with the wheel on the ground so that the bike's own weight keeps everything in place.

REPLACING SPOKES

Replacing a spoke is a straightforward operation, but it can be time consuming. Spokes will give little warning before they snap, and the usual causes are previous damage or uneven spoke tension due to rim damage or repeated heavy impacts. Most spoke failures are due to fatigue, so if one breaks the chances are the others are ready to follow suit. If you get repeated spoke failures, consider having the whole wheel rebuilt. Properly tensioned hand-built wheels are less likely to fail and they are a wise investment.

1 In emergencies, you can replace the spoke with the tyre in place, but only if you have exactly the right length of spoke. It's always best to remove the tyre, tube and rim tape so that you can access the nipple and replace it if necessary. Over-long spokes will protrude into the rim cavity and burst the tube so make sure you take care when picking the replacement spoke.

TOOLS REQUIRED

- **Spoke key**
- **Spare spokes (make sure you have the correct length)**
- **Screwdriver and/or nipple driver**
- **Truing stand**

2 If the spoke is outbound (the head of the spoke faces into the hub centre) you will have to thread the spoke in from the opposite side of the wheel. This is the easiest way to lace the spoke into the wheel.

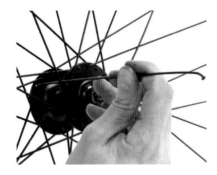

3 The spoke can pass through the lower part of the spokes on the opposite side of the wheel. The spoke will then usually travel over the first two crossing spokes and under the last one before reaching the rim.

4 Inbound spokes (where the head of the spoke faces out from the hub centre) are far more tricky to lace. You have to angle the spoke upwards so that it avoids the crossing at the other side of the wheel. Be careful not to bend the spoke too much as this will weaken it.

5 Spokes usually cross three times between the hub and the rim. Depending on the way the wheel has been laced, the spokes will cross under twice and over once or over twice and under once. Either way, it is essential that you copy this lacing when you replace a spoke to maintain the integrity and strength of the wheel.

6 In order to thread the spoke into the hole in the rim, you will have to push it under the rim. Protect the rim from being scratched by the threads when you do this by placing a finger or thumb over the end of the spoke, at the same time bending the spoke very gently and evenly so that it can tuck under the rim.

8 The correct length spoke will meet the rim eyelet and should be long enough to pass through the nipple and be level with the top of it on the inside of the rim. Any longer and the spoke will be too slack on the nipple. The nipple can be replaced if necessary; nipples can round off with poorly fitting spoke keys and poor-quality nipples can shear off.

10 Eyeletted rims last longer than non-eyeletted ones and experience fewer breakages as the eyelets allow the nipples to move slightly inside the rim. The eyelets also reinforce the rim and are easier to true as the nipples move freely inside them.

7 Here the replacement spoke is positioned behind the final crossing spoke and is long enough to insert into the rim cavity through the eyelet. If it won't reach the rim check that it crosses the other spokes correctly. You may need a longer spoke.

9 Take up the slack with a screwdriver before you start to true the wheel. Make a note of how far the other spokes protrude from the nipple and – if you have the correct length spoke – you can get the spoke to a similar position. See opposite for more on truing wheels.

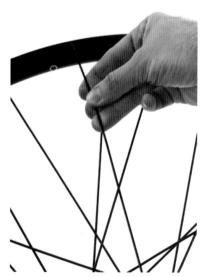

SPOKE TIPS

- Always have another wheel handy so you can copy the spoke pattern, especially if you are replacing more than one spoke.

- Use a nipple driver to run nipples onto the spoke threads. Stop when the nipple just reaches the end of the threaded section.

- Carefully bed in the elbows of the spokes by using either your thumb or the face of a plastic mallet.

- Use brass washers (DT make these) on loose spoke holes. Some wheel builders 'set' the nipples into the holes with a nail punch – be careful though when using bonded or lightweight hubs.

TRUING WHEELS

Wheel building is a great skill to acquire and very rewarding. This isn't the place to show you how to do it, though. Gerd Schraener's *The Art of Wheelbuilding* and Jobst Brandt's *The Bicycle Wheel* both offer excellent tuition and guidance in this process. Wheel building is involved rather than difficult, but the fact that there are complete books written on the subject speaks for itself. Here we'll show you the basics of wheel truing and hope you'll get the bug and want to learn more about how wheels are built.

First, assess the wheel and decide where the imbalance could be. Spin the wheel and see where the buckles are and where the wheel has uneven tension. A wheel is like a suspension bridge and any imbalance in the supports (spokes) places more stress on the neighbouring supports. The most common problem is a broken spoke, but spokes can also be loose or damaged, which will also cause a wobble.

When you spin the wheel, it should sit centrally in the jig (or bike if you are on the trail), so your job is to find out where, and more importantly how, the wheel is being pulled away from this centre line. Do not attempt to true a wheel until you have a good idea what is causing the buckle. Lateral (side-to-side) buckles are the easiest to solve:

TOOLS REQUIRED

- **Truing stand**
- **Spoke keys (there are a variety of nipple sizes depending on spoke type and gauge)**
- **Dishing stick**
- **Spoke tension meter (optional)**

- if the wheel bulges to the left, tighten the spoke on the right or loosen the spoke on the left;

- if the wheel bulges to the right, tighten the spoke on the left or loosen the spoke on the right.

However, radial (up and down) hops are a little different:

- if the hop is towards the hub, the spoke is too tight;

- if the hop is away from the hub, the spoke is too loose.

So, if the rim hops to the left and towards the hub at the same time, there is a spoke pulling too tightly on the left, and if the rim hops to the right and away from the hub at the same time, there is a loose spoke on the right.

That is the simple version. The rest is about practice and experience. The first few times you true a wheel it will take you some time, but if you can be patient (and practise) it will come as second nature. Remember to make small adjustments at first and mark the rim with chalk or wrap a strip of tape on the

suspect spokes so that you always know where you started.

Rear wheels have tighter spokes on the drive side than they do on the non-drive side. The non-drive spokes are also longer. This means that they require fewer turns than the drive side; it depends on the wheel but the ratio is about 2:1. On front hubs you will always need to loosen or tighten the same amount on both sides. Whatever you do, do it gradually and in no more than quarter- or half-turns at a time.

RIM HEALTH

Most rims designed for use with rim brakes have a wear indicator, which is either a black line or a series of dots on the middle of the rim. As the rim wears, these marks very slowly disappear, and when you can't see them anymore then the rim needs changing. It is very important to keep an eye on this, as the rims can wear severely and, combined with the pressure in the tyre, the bead on the rim will eventually fail. This can be catastrophic. The tube immediately explodes and the tyre is blown off the rim. The remaining part of the rim can easily tangle in the frame and, if it's the front wheel, you can have a very nasty accident. One of the main advantages of disc brakes is that rim wear is no longer an issue, although disc brakes do put big loads through wheels so the spoke tension needs to be spot on.

1 Treat the spokes in groups rather than individually. The usual cause of a buckle is a broken spoke (for more on replacing spokes see page 123); however, here we are trying to find the loose ones that may just require tightening. Grab several spokes at a time and squeeze them to feel where the problem is before you start to true the wheel.

2 Always use a spoke key that fits the nipples snugly. A loose-fitting key will ruin the nipple very easily, especially if the nipple is tight. If the spoke becomes very tight and the rim still needs to move some more, you may have to loosen the opposite spoke to allow a little more movement. Spokes tighten with a standard right-hand thread, so if you are using your right hand you will need to turn the spoke key towards you to tighten the spoke and away from you to loosen it.

3 A severe radial hop or a skip in the rim can signify a set or group of very loose or tight spokes. As with the lateral truing, you need careful judgement to decide which spokes to tackle first. Grab hold of a few and try to find the loose ones first. Then, using quarter-turns only, adjust the tension in two or four spokes at a time – you need to pull on both sides equally to prevent the wheel going out laterally as well as radially.

4 'Dish' describes the offset of the rim between the hub flanges. The flanges aren't symmetrical on rear wheels because there needs to be space for the cassette on one side. The rim needs to be equally spaced with the hub lock nuts (where the wheel is held in the frame or forks). Wheel dish is determined by measuring the wheel with a dishing stick, which checks that the lock nuts are equally spaced on either side of the rim.

TENSION

Even spoke tension is essential for a long-lasting wheel. Spokes with grossly different tensions from the rest are easy to detect by feel (remembering that the rear wheel drive-side spokes are roughly twice as tight as the non-drive-side ones). To pick up more subtle differences, professional wheel builders will use a spoke tension meter – this one is from DT Swiss. This can accurately measure spoke tension and enables a good wheel builder to keep variation in spoke tension to around 10 per cent. This is also useful when truing a wheel, as you can assess which spokes are being pushed too hard and are therefore likely to break first. If a wheel needs a big variation in tension to get it straight, it's likely that the rim has become permanently deformed – it's best to replace it if that's the case.

5 Rim dents and wear to the braking surfaces will make a difference to the tension in the wheel. Dents usually happen when the wheel pinch punctures due to hitting a root or a rock. Mountain bike wheels will absorb a lot of shock and the rims are made from very strong heat-treated alloys, so the chances are the rim will dent rather than collapse.

6 Accurate truing has to be done using a quality wheel jig rather than with the wheel still in the bike. Wheel jigs provide more stability, so the wheel doesn't rock around when you spin it. The wheel jig pictured here has self-centring jaws and retaining arms so that the rim will be perfect if it is trued to the guides. The jaws can be adjusted so that the rim drags on them to give you a visual and audible clue as to where the buckle is.

7 Once you are happy that the wheel is round again, 'stress' the wheel in your lap or gently on the floor. Do not stress the wheel with your full weight, especially if the bearings are sealed, as they are vulnerable to side loads. You will hear the wheel click and ping as the spokes 'find' their position. This may mean that the rim moves a little, so double-check it in the jig before you're finished.

8 Finally, replace the rim tape. Always use tape that sticks to the rim; this way you know it will not come loose and move around under the tube. Plastic tape is better than cloth as cloth tape holds water and will rust the eyelets, which in turn can seize the nipples. Rim tape should be renewed every time it is removed – never re-use old tape.

RIM REPLACEMENT

Replacing a rim on an existing wheel is a good step towards building a wheel from scratch. If the old rim is worn or dented but the spokes are in good condition, simply tape the new rim alongside the old one, making sure that the valve holes are level and it's aligned the same way – spoke holes are staggered left and right. Loosen all the spokes, then move them one at a time from the old rim to the new one. Discard the old rim. Tighten all the spokes evenly, working methodically around the rim. As they begin to get tight, start to work on hops and wobbles as per wheel truing. Tighten all the spokes evenly if it's straight. Compare with a known good wheel to get the tension right.

HUBS

CUP AND CONE BEARINGS

Traditional cup and cone bearing hubs are very simple to service. The first few times can be challenging, but experience really speeds the process up. The key is to make sure that all the components are in top condition – any wear and tear to the cones or bearings means that the parts should be replaced.

Hubs will need a complete service every four to six months depending on weather conditions and how often you ride. Fresh grease and regular adjustment will keep hubs rolling for a long time. Shimano cone hubs are excellent because you can rebuild them very easily and quickly and they use top-quality bearings and hardened steel cones. Look after them properly and they'll last almost indefinitely.

Loose hubs do not last very long. Grab your wheel by the tyre and shake the wheel from side to side while it is still in the bike. If you feel a slight knock or 'play' through the tyre, the hub is loose. This means that the bearings are bashing around inside the hub and slowly disintegrating, and the seals are more exposed, allowing water and muck into the hub. Leave the hub like this and it won't take long for the internals to fail completely. Rebuilding the wheel with a new hub is far more costly and time-consuming than replacing the grease and the bearings every few months.

TOOLS REQUIRED

- **2 x 13mm cone spanners (Shimano use 13mm cones, but they can vary in size)**
- **Torque wrench**
- **17mm open-ended spanner (or cone spanner)**
- **Grease**
- **Axle vice and bench-mounted vice**

FRONT HUBS

1 The key to easy hub servicing is only working on one side. If you keep one side intact, the spacing over the lock nuts is easier to retain. A standard QR front hub measures 100mm between the faces of the locknuts. This measurement is critical so that the wheel can easily be replaced in the forks. Through-axle hubs are 110mm wide.

2 Cone spanners are very thin and flat. This means that they can fit into the machined flats on the sides of the cone and can adjust and tighten the cones without snagging on the washer and lock-nut. Use the correct size and don't use cone spanners to remove your pedals, as this will damage them. Hold the cone with a cone spanner and release the lock nut with a 17mm spanner.

3 Undo and remove the lock nut, then the washer and, finally, the cone. The cone is made from hardened steel and has a highly polished bearing surface. Inspect the cone carefully for any rough patches on the surface, which is known as pitting. On most front wheels there is only a cone, washer and lock nut.

GREASE

Every mechanic has a favourite hub grease. The secret is to use a specially formulated synthetic bicycle grease that is waterproof and of a consistent quality, but also not to overdo it as this can make the bearings drag and adjustment more difficult. Many of the non-synthetic or engineering-type greases are too heavy for hub bearings. Also, avoid lithium (usually white-coloured) grease, as it is easily washed out of the bearings and breaks down after repeated revolutions. Shimano hub grease is excellent as is Finish Line, Park, Pedros and Rock 'n' Roll. Use a grease gun with a fine nozzle to direct grease where you want it; this will avoid waste.

4 Remove the cone, spacers and – very carefully – the axle. It's best to do this over something that will catch the bearings should they fall out. Place the threaded components down on the workbench or over an Allen key in the order they came off the hub to help you remember the order to return them. Clean the axle and cones, leaving one side on the axle and in one piece. Keep all

the bearings so that you can check you are replacing the same size and quantity.

5 Clean the inside of the bearing surfaces and inspect for damage. If the bearing surfaces and cones are pitted, you will need to replace either the cones or the hub assembly. Replacing the cones and the bearings and resetting them in grease will usually solve any hub roughness.

6 You don't have to remove the hub seals – they're factory fitted and are very hard to replace properly as they are pressed into the shell of the hub, and it is possible to see into the hub with the seals in place. However, if you do have to remove them, be very careful. Wrap a rag around a tyre lever and prise the seals out carefully. Don't use a screwdriver as they can bend the seal, and if that happens you'll never get it back in again.

To replace the seal, use your fingers to locate it and then tap it home using a rubber mallet.

7 It is good practice to replace the bearings after every strip down. The bearings are slightly more vulnerable than the cones and the hub surfaces, so they tend to wear out first. Look at them closely and you will see tiny potholes. Bearings need to be mirror finished, so if they are even slightly dull they need replacing. It's useful to have a magnetic screwdriver for this job, as it makes re-installation far easier. Store spare bearings on a magnet to make them easier to manage.

8 When all the bearings are installed, take the loose cone and push it back into the hub. Rotate it a couple of times to seat the bearings. This will also tell you if there is any damage to the bearing surface inside

▶

the hub, and will stick the bearings in place so you can turn the wheel over to do the other side. Next, double-check that there are the right amount of bearings in the hub. Lastly, smear a little more grease on top of the bearings and check there isn't any grease inside the hub. You will then be able to push the axle through without making a big mess.

9 Replace the axle (remember to return it in the same way it was removed). As you have only disturbed one set of bearings, the spacing will not have been altered. Screw the cone onto the axle and up to the bearings. Spin the axle in your fingers and 'rock' it slightly from side to side – you are looking for the point at which there is no 'play', only smooth spinning. When you are happy that the bearings are running smoothly, replace the washer and then the lock nut. At this stage they need to be finger tight.

10 With practice, you will be able to set the cones like this and simply do up the cone as in step 2. However, when you tighten the lock nut for the last time, you may also either loosen the cone slightly or tighten it. Mountain bike hubs have seals in the hub body that will drag a little when the cone is set. To set the cones properly you will need two cone spanners (13mm for front hubs); with two spanners you can work the cones against each other. So, if you over-tighten the lock nut, place the two cone spanners on either side of the hub and slightly undo the cones until the axle spins freely.

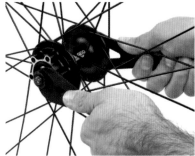

HUB TIPS

Replace the wheel into the bike and check for play by rocking the wheel from side to side. Then pick up the bike and spin the wheel quickly. Hold onto either fork leg. You may feel a rumbling of vibration through the fork, in which case the cones are too tight. Re-check the cones again after your first ride.

Using an axle vice to hold the wheel steady will help if your hub isn't built into a wheel, but isn't necessary if the wheel is complete. Axle vices are made from a soft material and clamp the axle tightly so you can work on the hub with both hands, which will speed things up. The best way to work on a hub as a part of the wheel is on top of a workbench with the hub at a slight angle so you can see into the internals.

REAR HUBS

Much of the information in the front hub section (see pages 128-130) applies to rear hubs too. The bearings are assembled in the same way, although many of the dimensions are different. Rear hubs also contain the freehub mechanism, which can be replaced.

Rear hub spacing is usually 135mm across the lock nuts for a quick-release hub. Through axle systems with 142mm hubs are becoming more common, and some freeride and downhill bikes have 150mm rear ends.

If both cones need to be replaced, it is worth measuring the position of the lock nut and cones before you start work. Measure the distance from the end of the axle to the side of the first lock nut. Then, when you start to remove the cones, work on one side at a time and place the components down in the order that they are removed. Thread them over a screwdriver or an Allen key in reverse order so they don't get muddled.

Before you start, remove the cassette as described on page 70.

TOOLS REQUIRED

- **Cone spanners (the Shimano rear hub has 15mm cones, but they do vary in size)**
- **17mm open-ended spanner (or cone spanner)**
- **10mm Allen key**
- **Grease**
- **Axle vice and bench-mounted vice**
- **Cassette service and replacement tools**
- **Chain whip**
- **Cassette lock ring tool and spanner/wrench**
- **Torque wrench**

1 Work on the non-drive side first. Remove the rubber cover and undo the lock nut. As with the front hub, leave the drive side intact to ensure that the spacing remains identical – this is especially important with the rear hub as uneven spacing can affect the chainline and the gear shifting.

2 As with the front hubs, set all the axle components to one side and clean the hub bearing surfaces. When the hub is cleaned, remove the cassette body with a 10mm Allen key. The cassette body is usually factory fitted and tight, so you will need an appropriate Allen key (a long one). You may need to use a pipe for a little extra leverage to undo the bolt.

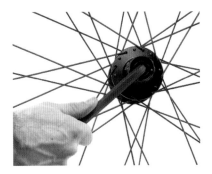

3 The bolt that retains the cassette body can be fully removed and the cassette body can be replaced if necessary. To refit, locate the cassette body on the splines on the end of the hub. Be careful not to lose the washer that sits on the inside of the body. Set the torque wrench to 34.3–49Nm and tighten the bolt.

▶ **4** Grease and reset the bearings into the hub. Nine 1/4in bearings are usually required, but, as with the front hub, double-check that you are returning the same amount as you removed. It is impossible to detect damage to the surface of the bearings, so new ones must be used to ensure smooth running. Take your time and set the bearings in grease so that they are covered and the grease is worked in.

5 The grease will be enough to hold the bearings in place. Insert the axle, with the drive-side spacers and cones still in place, from the drive side. It is best to do this over the bench in case the bearings decide to escape.

6 Spin the non-drive side cone onto the axle and set the cone finger tight. Add any spacers and washers and finally the lock nut, then set the cones. This is harder with the rear hub because the drive-side cone is tucked into the cassette body. It is therefore far easier to do this job with the wheel secured in an axle vice, and some mechanics even adjust the hub when it is back in the bike. However, this requires experience. Lastly, return any rubber covers and you will then be able to reinstall the cassette.

LUBRICATING FREEHUB BODIES

As the freehub mechanism wears it can start to stick or slip. Sometimes they can be rescued by soaking them in release agent (paraffin or diesel fuel) overnight. You can also try dribbling light oil through them from the top. This won't cure long-term problems, but will shift the muck from the mechanism and can keep it going for a little longer. If you've gone to the trouble of stripping the hub and removing the freehub body, though, you might as well play safe and replace it.

CARTRIDGE BEARINGS

Unlike adjustable cup and cone style hubs, cartridge bearing hubs rely on a sealed bearing unit that can be removed and replaced. The bearings are set into a hardened steel cartridge that press-fits into the hub shell or freehub body. This unit is packed with grease and sealed with plastic or labyrinth seals. The quality is determined by the number of bearings and amount of grease packed into them. Once the bearing is pushed into the hub, the axle can be pushed tightly into the bearings. This gives you a smooth spinning feel, as there is less chance of over-tightening the bearing with lock nuts and cones.

The obvious advantage of sealed bearings is that they require less adjustment and servicing than standard cup and cone bearings. However, they are only as good as the quality of bearings and standard of engineering of the hub shells. A cartridge hub at the cheaper end of the range may have push-fit covers and less sealing than a Shimano cup and cone hub.

Sealed bearings do not like side loads and can be easily damaged, so always treat them with care and always use the manufacturer's recommended tools to remove them.

The following method for fitting new bearings in hubs with cartridge units is fairly straightforward. Each manufacturer will have its own tools and bearings, but the general principle is fairly standard.

TOOLS REQUIRED

- **Plastic mallet**
- **Bearing fitting dies**
- **Allen keys**
- **Cleaning kit**
- **Grease**
- **Cone spanner**

1 The spacers at the end of each side of the axle are either push-fit or locked into place with a threaded lock ring. Sometimes a grub screw can lock them in place. The ones shown here require an Allen key and a cone spanner to undo the cassette-retaining spacer.

2 This non-drive-side spacer threads onto the axle end. Many (like Hope) are a simple push-on fitting. The key here is the quality of the fit between the axle and the

bearing, as this is what takes the strain. Oversize axles are a good idea with sealed bearings as they can handle much more abuse and tend to twist less under load.

3 With the spacers and lock nuts removed, the cassette body can be taken off. On most cartridge hubs the cassette will be a push-fit secured by the drive-side spacer. However, some, like this Bontrager wheel, use a Shimano-type freewheel that is bolted to the hub body. You will need a 10mm Allen key to remove this.

4 Push out the old cartridge bearings. This Bontrager wheel's axle has to be tapped out with a plastic mallet. Once one side has been removed, the cartridge will pop out, still attached to the axle.

5 This Bontrager hub has a bolt-on cassette body and is removed in the same way as a Shimano hub (see step 3) with a 10mm Allen key. You can see the collar that holds the cartridge bearing. This needs to be cleaned thoroughly before a new bearing can be installed.

6 The remaining bearing on the axle can be tapped off by placing the axle in a die. This allows you to use the axle as a drift to remove the remaining bearing on the other side of the hub. To replace the bearing you will have to place it on top of the die and tap the axle back in. When it is flush to the shoulder in the centre of the axle, it is ready to be re-installed to the hub.

7 The new bearings can be replaced. All sealed bearings have a code number and can be bought at most engineering suppliers or your local bike shop.

8 Use an appropriate die to seat the new bearings into the hub. They are a tight fit, but must be installed gently so as not to damage the bearing unit or the seals. Press in the new bearings with care. Put some grease around the outside of the bearing and place it square onto the hub. Use an insertion tool that is the same size as the outer part of the bearing. Any side load onto the plastic seal part of the bearing will ruin it. Tap the bearing home.

CARTRIDGE BEARING TIPS

- With care, the seals can be removed with a scalpel blade and the old grease flushed out with degreaser. Use a grease gun to inject fresh grease into the bearings inside the collars.

- Avoid solvent-based lubricants on sealed bearing hubs as they can damage the seals and flush out the grease from the bearings.

9 Most cartridge bearing hubs have their own type of cassette. They usually pull off once the lock rings and spacers have been removed. Inside the hub is a series of teeth and on the cassette body are three sprung pawls. These pawls engage with the teeth when you pedal and 'click' around freely when you stop pedalling. The hub pictured here has one circular spring that holds the pawls in place.

10 Here you can see the serrated part inside the hub. This needs to be completely cleaned out and lightly greased before you replace the rebuilt cassette body.

11 Carefully remove the pawls and clean all the dirty grease off the cassette body. Use a toothbrush to clean out all the pawl indentations and spring channels.

12 The cassette shown here has a single circular spring, so the pawls need to be set in grease and then have the spring replaced over them. This does take time as it's quite fiddly. Many hubs have springs for individual pawls. If these fail they will need replacing as they can get stuck into the serrated parts and ruin the freewheel.

13 Use a light-weight grease on the freehubs. Heavy grease tends to drag inside the hub, which can make the chain sag. To replace the cassette body you will need to push the pawls into the cassette body so it can fit into the hub. Some hubs supply a tool for this. Once the pawls are tucked away, the cassette body should pop into place. Double-check that it rotates freely before you rebuild the rest of the hub.

10

TYRES

Tyres are one of the favourite topics of mountain bike conversation, with 'What tyres for...?' being one of the most frequently asked questions. Tyres are one of the fundamental bike parts. You can do without gears or suspension, but you won't get far without tyres. Your tyres have to transfer all your inputs to the ground. The rear tyre has to use your pedalling efforts to push the bike along. The front tyre has to deal with most of the braking and steering. We expect our tyres to work in a spectacular range of conditions, from wet and muddy to dry and dusty. While the differences between tyres can be subtle, there are certainly differences, and a bad choice could spoil your ride.

With no moving parts, the maintenance requirements of tyres are relatively minimal. Keep them clean and correctly inflated and check them carefully for rips, tears or excessive wear. The main issue you're likely to face is, of course, punctures. With modern tubeless tyres it may be a long time before you experience one, but it's best to be prepared. With practice, a puncture can be repaired in a few minutes so the possibility should hold no fear.

CHOOSING TYRES

SIZE

There are now three tyre sizes in circulation. 26in tyres are the original size and have dominated for many years. 29in tyres, mounted on the same diameter rims as road bikes, are becoming increasingly popular, with some manufacturers moving almost entirely to 29ers for parts of their ranges. The bigger wheels roll more easily over bumps and have a longer, narrower contact patch that can be helpful under certain circumstances. The downside is a small weight penalty. It took bike designers a while to work out how to build frames to work with bigger wheels, but 29er frame geometry is reasonably well established now.

There's also 650B, which fits between 26 and 29in and claims to offer the best elements of both. 650B is easier to accommodate in full-suspension designs than 29in while still offering some fast-rolling benefits over 26in. 650B bikes are rare at the time of writing, but a number of large manufacturers are backing the size.

The other aspect of size is width. Mountain bike tyres can range from 1.5in (the minimum for use in races) up to 2.5in, with specific snow bikes able to accommodate 4in tyres. That's something of a niche, though. Measuring tyre width is a somewhat inexact science. There are industry standards, but everybody seems to ignore them and uses their own methods for measuring instead. The result is

that three tyres labelled 2.2in, 2.3in and 2.35in could easily be the same width. Make sure that there's room in your frame for larger tyres, too.

The European Tyre and Rim Technical Organisation (ETRTO) and the International Standards Organisation (ISO) use the same method to determine tyre width: take the distance between the two beads, measured over the tyre tread, and divide it by 2.5. However, some manufacturers take the measurement on the casing side from the edge of the bead to the centre of the casing, thus some of their tyres can look larger as they use the same casing volume but larger treads.

BEADS

All tyres have a bead that runs around the edge of the tyre and secures the tyre by locking under the lip of the rim. Steel beads keep a circular shape and Kevlar beads are flexible (and foldable), but both have similar strength. Steel beads are yielding enough to be stretched onto a rim; Kevlar doesn't stretch so the beads are made a bit longer, which helps but can make the procedure a bit of a handful, with a half-mounted tyre flopping about the place. Kevlar-beaded tyres are substantially lighter, although also more expensive.

COMPOUNDS

Coloured tyres have come and gone over the years. At the moment tyres are generally black, but most are available in a range of compounds. Tyre hardness is measured on the Shore hardness

---

CASING

Tyre casings are made from nylon cloth, with the threads oriented diagonally. Finer threads, denoted by a higher threads per inch (TPI) value, give a lighter and more supple casing that should deliver better grip. Casings may contain reinforcement to ward off punctures or increase the stiffness of the sidewall to allow lower pressures to be used.

---

scale, with bigger numbers harder. A 50a is quite a hard compound, a 42a somewhat soft. Soft compounds give better grip on hard surfaces like rocks, but they wear more quickly and feel draggier. Hard compounds last longer but don't grip as well in conditions where you're relying on the properties of the tyre rubber rather than the shape of the tread.

TREAD

There are hundreds of different tread patterns available, and it's easy to become bewildered by the choice. They tend to fall into a few obvious categories, though. Very shallow treads with lots of low-profile, closely spaced blocks work best in dry, hard conditions. Deep treads with tall, narrow, widely-spaced blocks are effective in mud. Between the two are all-rounders – medium height treads with some space between them but not as much as the mud tyre. We find that tyres with simple, squarish blocks staggered across the width of the casing work well under most conditions. There are lots of tyres like this, and they're a good choice if you don't know exactly what you're going to encounter. Everybody has their personal favourite, so try out as many as you can and use a tread pattern that suits your type of riding.

Most tyres can be used on the front or rear, although some are more suitable for one end of the bike than the other. You'll usually find directional arrows on tyres too, indicating which way round they should be fitted. Sometimes this will be different for front or rear usage. Some tyres are symmetrical and can be run either way.

PRESSURE

Tyre pressure for mountain bikes is often overlooked, but it can have a major effect on the handling and stability of your bike. Mountain bike tyres can be used with a wide range of pressures, from under 20 to over 60psi depending on the tyres. Very large tyres on snow bikes can be run at single-digit

pressures. High pressures give a fast ride on hard surfaces but at the expense of comfort and grip. Low pressures give lots of traction but can become draggy. Very low pressures lead to soggy sidewalls and poor cornering, as well as a high risk of impact punctures.

You can afford to use higher pressures with suspension bikes as the travel will eat up the shock, but if you ride with rigid forks you will need to take more care. Look at the recommended pressures on the sidewall of the tyre and stick within the limits. Experiment with different conditions and pressures – try harder, narrower tyres for fast conditions and mud and softer, wider tyres for technical conditions or when you need more grip.

REPAIRING A PUNCTURE

Punctures are a fact of mountain biking life. The vast majority of mountain bikes still use traditional inner tubes, although tubeless tyres are growing in popularity.

While inner tubes are relatively cheap, puncture repair patches are cheaper. If you ride in the autumn, when the hedges are clipped and there are therefore more thorns on the trail, or in the wet when flints and sharp grit are washed into the trail, you can expect several flats – the cost of using a new tube each time can mount up.

That said, it's far better to replace the tube than try to patch it if you are out on the trail. Who wants to wait for the glue to go off, try to keep the patches dry and try to sand some French chalk if it's snowing? Fixing tubes is best done in the dry as it can take around ten minutes to mend each hole. Carry a spare tube (or two), use them if you need to and repair the punctured one at home. If you use a decent puncture kit it's highly unlikely that the patch will leak; in fact, Rema feathered-edge patches are stronger than the tube itself. A patched tube is essentially as good as new.

REMOVING A TYRE

Most tubed tyres can be removed without the use of tyre levers, although sometimes you'll encounter a really tight combination of tyre and rim that just won't shift any other way. Tubeless-ready rims and tyres are usually a tighter fit, and if you're using a tubeless conversion that relies on a thick rim tape to seal the spoke holes you may find that that makes things more difficult too. Out on the trail, with potentially cold, wet hands, it's often easier to use levers – see page 180 for trailside tyre removal.

1 If you've had a puncture the tyre will be flat already, but take the valve cap off and compress the valve core to let any remaining air out. If the tyre is fully inflated the air will come out quite quickly. Remove the valve lock ring. Work around the tyre and pop the beads inwards from the rim.

2 Starting opposite the valve, squeeze the tyre beads together and push them right down into the well of the rim. By pushing them down on one side of the rim you should be able to get enough slack to push the beads off at the opposite side of the rim.

3 Work your hands outwards, pushing the slack in the tyre around the rim with your thumbs. Keep the pressure on so that you're pulling the top bit of the tyre into the rim. It helps to rest the top edge of the rim against your legs to keep the tyre pushed in.

4 When your hands meet at the opposite side of the wheel, the beads should be clear of the lip of the rim and can be pulled off. If they're not quite there, try the procedure again. You may have to resort to tyre levers – often just one will do it.

5 Once you've got a few inches of bead clear, run a tyre lever (or finger, but take care in case there are thorns or flint in there) around the rest of the bead to lift it off the rim. Once one bead is off it's usually easy to pop the other one off.

6 Remove the inner tube. Make sure you check the inside of the tyre thoroughly for thorns before putting a new or repaired inner tube in. It's annoying to repair a puncture only for it to go down again instantly.

PATCHING AN INNER TUBE

1 Find the hole. This is usually a case of pumping up the tube and listening. Just keep pumping until you hear the hiss. Failing that, pump the tube up and look closely at it all the way around – you might not see the hole but you'll feel the air coming out. Really tiny holes might only be discovered by dunking the tube in a bowl of water. Once you have the hole, place your finger and thumb over it as you don't want to lose it.

2 Roughen up the area around the hole with some sandpaper. This will help the glue penetrate the rubber and ensure the patch adheres properly. The glue is a contact adhesive (it works when the patch is placed on it), but needs to be applied to a grease-free and dry tube in order to work properly.

TOOLS REQUIRED

- **Pump**
- **Sandpaper**
- **Glue**
- **Patch**
- **French chalk or talc (optional)**

3 Apply plenty of glue to the area, starting at the hole and working outwards. Keep an eye on where the hole is so you can get the patch over it properly later on. Leave the glue for five minutes until it is almost completely dry.

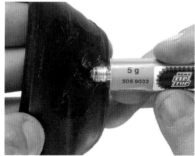

4 Most fixable holes can be covered by a 2cm patch. If it's a pinch flat (or snakebite puncture – see page 144) use two patches (one over each hole) rather than one big one. Apply firm pressure to the patch with your

thumb, as you want the patch to be fully in place before you re-inflate. To guarantee good adhesion, put something heavy on the patch and leave it for a while.

5 Remove the plastic backing film from the centre. It's usually perforated in the middle and will split if you bend the tube. Don't pull it off from a corner as it can pull the patch off with it. The backing is used to make sure you don't touch the underside of the patch and so you can press it onto the tube easily.

6 If you can dust the area with French chalk or talc, this will prevent the glue from sticking to the inside of the tyre carcass and help it slide into place as you inflate the tyre. It's good practice to lightly dust the whole tube with talc so it can move slightly inside the tyre.

REFITTING THE TYRE AND TYRE

1 Put one tyre bead onto the rim, taking careful note of the orientation of the tyre – if there are directional arrows on it, make sure they're going the right way. Allow the bead to sit in the well of the rim.

2 Pump the inner tube up just enough for it to hold its shape so it's less likely to get pinched. Push the valve through the hole in the rim and pop the partially inflated tube into the tyre all the way round

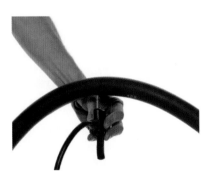

3 Starting opposite the valve, hook the other bead into the rim. The procedure is very similar to taking the tyre off – apply pressure around the tyre, engaging the bead as you go and trying to generate enough slack to pop the last bit on.

4 By the time your hands meet at the far side of the tyre, you should be able to push the last bit of bead over the rim with your thumbs. If it's almost there but not quite, work around from the valve side again. Very snug tyres may need some encouragement from a tyre lever.

5 Replace the locking nut on the valve stem. Undo the small locking tip of the valve (Presta type only). Free it up by pressing it in a couple of times; this will enable the valve to pass air in easily as sometimes it gets 'stuck' after full inflation.

6 Push the pump head firmly onto the valve. Sometimes you will have to place a thumb behind the tyre to prevent the valve vanishing into the hole as you push it home (some valves have lock rings to prevent this).

7 All good pumps have a locking lever. This ensures that the pump head makes an airtight seal over the valve and means you can concentrate on inflating the tyre. The valve internals can be removed and replaced as they wear out. The seal can also be swapped around to cope with either valve type (see your pump instructions as this depends on the make).

8 Pump firmly but don't rush. If you push too hard or at an awkward angle you can bend the valve or snap the locking part off. Use all of the pumping stroke and take your time. Make sure there's adequate air pressure in the tyre before riding it again. Some tyres need inflating to their maximum pressure to properly seat themselves on the rim – let them slightly down again from there for riding.

TROUBLESHOOTER

If the tyre is leaking rapidly, check the following:

- Gashes in the sidewall, even if they don't go through the tyre completely, can leak slowly and will reduce the performance of the tyre. Have a good look around the whole tyre and patch any that may seem suspect.

- Check the bead seating. Inflate the tyre to 10 per cent more than the maximum recommended pressure. Then deflate the tyre completely. The bead should remain firmly tucked into the rim edge and retain the seal. If it doesn't, the bead may be damaged.

- Clean the rim and bead with soapy water and replace the tyre as recommended.

- Check the rims for dents or scratches.

- Lastly, if these tips don't help, inflate the tyre to about 50 PSI and submerge it in the bath. Any holes will show up pretty quickly.

TYRE BOOT

Large tyre gashes need to be repaired because the tube will blister out of any holes in the tyre carcass and explode again. You can use an empty energy gel packet or a piece of cardboard to cover the hole, but proper tyre boots are better as they stick to the inside of the tyre and don't slip as you re-inflate it.

'GLUELESS' PATCHES

Although not as permanent as the glue and patch variety, glueless patches can provide an emergency fix and work especially well if you are in a rush or if it's raining, as you don't have to wait for the glue to dry. As with standard patches, sand the area properly to help the patch fix to the tube.

SNAKEBITE PUNCTURES

Snakebite punctures occur when you have smacked something pretty hard (usually a stone, slate or sharp tree root) and the tube is pinched between the object and the rim, making two holes on either rim edge – hence 'snakebite' as it looks like two teeth have punctured your tube. These are hard to fix as you will usually need two patches – one to cover each hole.

VALVE TYPES

There are two types of tyre valve in common use. Presta valves (the thin ones) require you to unscrew the centre before inflating, while Schrader valves (the fatter car-style ones) open by themselves. Presta is less leak prone and requires a smaller hole in the rim, while Schrader tubes can be inflated with car pumps or garage air lines (although many garages don't like you doing this). If your rims are drilled for the larger Schrader valves, fit plastic grommets to reduce the holes for Presta to prevent the valves from moving around and possibly getting damaged.

TUBELESS TYRES

There are two main types of tubeless tyre in circulation. UST tyres, a standard developed by rim manufacturer Mavic and tyre manufacturers Michelin and Hutchinson, have a specially shaped locking bead and an extra layer of rubber on the inside of the casing to make them airtight. This extra rubber adds weight, which led to the development of tubeless-ready tyres. These also have a locking bead but with a normal casing. They rely on a liquid sealant to hold air. Both types of tyre should be used with the appropriate rims, equipped with correctly profiled bead hooks. The rims will either be sealed by design, with no spoke holes on the inside of the rim bed, or will use a special rim strip to seal the holes. Not all tubeless-ready rims have the UST logo, but if they're described as tubeless-ready they'll have locking beads. Typically tubeless-ready tyres can be used on UST rims as well as tubeless-ready ones, but you may have trouble with UST tyres on tubeless-ready rims – some combinations are a very tight fit.

There are also tubeless conversion kits that use a thick sealed rim strip and valve to turn conventional rims into tubeless. The thickness of the strip helps the tyre bead to lock into the rim, but can make it harder to fit tyres. It's sometimes possible to use conventional tyres without tubes on UST, tubeless-ready or converted rims, but it very much depends on the tyre – there are no guarantees.

Regardless of the exact system, tubeless tyres offer greater puncture resistance than tubes and can be run at lower pressures before pinch flats become a problem. Tubeless-ready setups with sealant are lighter than tubes, too.

FITTING TUBELESS TYRES

1 UST double-walled rims are sealed, with no access to the spoke nipples through the inside of the rim. The nipples are oversized and thread directly into the rim. This means you will have to true the wheel with this special spoke key, but also means that you can replace a spoke without having to remove the tyres.

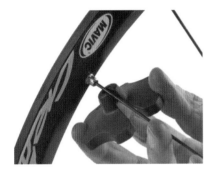

2 UST tyres are a little heavier than standard tyres, with a more substantial sidewall and a fatter bead. As with a standard tyre you will need to check the direction arrows on the side wall. You must only use ETRTO-compatible tyres, but most of the main manufacturers have a UST option to their ranges. Tubeless-ready tyres with sealant are a lighter option.

TOOLS REQUIRED

- **Soapy water to help seal the tyre to the rim**
- **A decent track pump**
- **Plastic tyre levers – definitely don't use metal ones**

3 The valve is the key element to the tubeless wheel. It's recommended that you replace the valve periodically. This valve is for a sealed rim – some tubeless-ready rims require a rim tape with a built-in valve, and a similar arrangement is used for tubeless conversion kits.

4 The rubber flange of the valve has to sit inside the well in the middle of the rim. A little soapy water or Vaseline on the rubber seal will help seal the valve and the rim. Here you can see the well that runs around the base of the rim – this helps to install the tyre bead. Also notice the absence of spoke holes.

5 There is an O-ring that fits over the valve to seal it to the rim. Check that this is in place over the join between the rim and the valve, and replace it on a regular basis. Moisten it slightly with some Vaseline to help it seal the air in completely.

6 The lock ring is tightened on top of the O-ring. This should only be done up finger tight. It is possible to fit a Schrader valve adaptor to the Presta-size valve, but the UST system can only be used with the UST valve. Some valves for tubeless-ready systems have removable cores to allow sealant to be injected through them.

7 Soap the rim with some very diluted soapy water. Then, starting opposite the valve hole, place one side of the tyre bead over the rim and into the well in the middle of the rim. If you push the bead into this well, it makes it far easier to pull the tyre onto the rim as it adds some slack to the bead. Work with both hands around the rim towards the valve hole. Do not be tempted to use tyre levers; the tyre should go on with minimal force.

8 Once one side of the tyre is on, push the bead to the side of the well so that there's space for the other bead. Run your finger around the well inside the rim and push the bead firmly towards the other side of the rim. Then, starting opposite the valve hole again, insert the second bead, forcing it into the well again so that once you reach the valve hole there will be enough slack to pull the tyre on easily.

9 Pulling the final bit on is tricky, so be careful not to damage the tyre bead at this point. You may have to force the tyre on a little, but if the bead has been placed into the well correctly it should be pretty easy. If the tyre is too tight, work both sides of the wheel around to the valve hole until there is a small amount left to pull on. You may need to add a little more soapy water to assist this bit.

10 If you're using a tubeless-ready tyre and the valve core isn't removable, add sealant directly into the tyre before engaging the last part of the bead. You don't need much – 40-100g should be ample. Tyre sealant is latex based, with various different added ingredients depending on the brand.

11 It should be possible to inflate a tubeless setup with an ordinary track pump, although you may have to be quick with the first few pumps. The theory is that there'll be a good enough seal between the tyre and the rim bed to hold sufficient air pressure to force the beads out to the bead locks on the rim. Keep pumping until the tyre pops into the rim.

12 If air comes out as fast as you can put it in, try a bit more soapy water and make sure the tyre is on the rim evenly all the way round. You may need to use a compressor, or pop a tube in just to engage the beads – once they've 'popped', release one side sufficiently to get the tube out. With one bead engaged it should be easier to get the other one to go. Once the beads are engaged, adjust air pressure as desired.

REMOVING A TUBELESS TYRE

Because UST and tubeless-ready tyres rely on a locking bead, they can be hard to remove. Let all the air out and push the tyre bead inwards until it pops out. You may be able to do this with your thumbs, but if that doesn't work try pushing with the heel of your hand. Disengage all of one side first, then the other. Then work the slack around the rim and unhook it by the valve.

USING A STANDARD TUBE WITH A TUBELESS TYRE

The inner rubber layer of a UST tyre will cope with small punctures, and sealant deals with them too. If you get a hole too big for the tubeless setup to cope with, you'll get a flat tyre. UST tyres can be repaired by patching the inside of the tyre. There are several products especially made for this, including pre-glued patches, which will get you home if you puncture on the trail. The best bet is to carry a tube for emergency use – it's quicker than an in-the-field repair.

Only use a tube with a Presta valve. Drilling out a tubeless rim to take Schrader will mean that it won't seal properly.

TYRE TIPS

- If you use the same tyre on the front and rear wheels, swap them around regularly. This will help your tyres last longer as the rear tyre wears faster than the front.

- For races, consider carrying a partially inflated tube in a jersey pocket to save valuable seconds in the event of a puncture.

- Many racers practise fixing a flat, as punctures can mean losing important time and therefore races. World Cup riders can fix a flat in well under a minute, which is pretty good going – how quickly can you fix one?

- Think carefully about your needs when selecting tyres. Semi-slicks are going to be useless in the mud and lightweight cross-country tyres won't last long on an enthusiastically ridden freeride bike. As a rule, use fat tyres with plenty of tread. They last longer, puncture less and are far more comfortable than skinny ones.

- Tyre moulds are coated with release agent so that the freshly made tyres don't stick. This tends to remain on the outside of the tyre, and as you'd expect it's quite slippery. Take care for the first few miles on new tyres, they can be unpredictable until the release agent has rubbed off.

SUSPENSION

The purpose of mountain bike suspension is twofold. First, by isolating the rider from bumps, comfort is improved and fatigue reduced. Second, suspension maintains contact between the wheels and the ground, improving traction and control. All bike suspension is adjustable to a degree, and some systems are adjustable to the point of bewilderment. Suspension needs to be adjusted based not only on your weight but also to accommodate different riding styles. A racer is likely to run suspension harder and with faster rebound than a recreational rider, who's likely to be more interested in comfort. In this book we won't be going into the nuances of each particular suspension configuration, as there are too many of them and they are constantly changing in terms of design and setup. So instead we will concentrate on the fundamentals of any suspension setup: damping and spring rate. Damping controls how quickly the shock or fork compresses or rebounds, while the spring rate suspends the rider and determines how much the suspension compresses under the combined weight of the bike and rider. Some experimentation is needed to find a set-up that suits you – we'll give you a good starting point in this chapter.

SUSPENSION FORK ANATOMY

STEERER TUBE

The steerer tube is a butted aluminium or steel threadless tube that connects the fork to the frame via the headset. Tapered steerers with different size bearings top and bottom are increasingly common.

1 CROWN

The crown is a key structural part, connecting the two stanchion tubes to the steerer tube. Usually made of forged aluminium and often hollow to save weight. Stanchions and steerer are usually press-fitted and not removable.

2 STANCHIONS

The upper fixed tubes of the fork. 32mm is the standard diameter for all-round forks, with steel stanchions on budget forks and aluminium with a hard surface coating at the higher end. Budget forks often have 28mm stanchions and you'll find 36 and 40mm for heavy-duty freeride and downhill forks.

3 WIPER SEALS

These push dirt and water off the stanchions as the forks compress to prevent them getting inside. Many forks have lubricated foam rings under the wiper seals to keep the stanchions lubricated, with oil seals underneath those.

4 LOWERS

All but the cheapest forks have lightweight cast magnesium lowers that move up and down over bumps. The lowers comprise

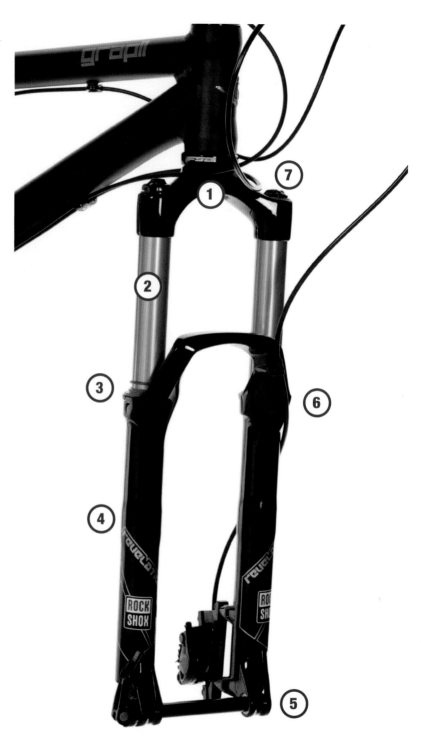

two legs joined by a brace to keep them moving together. The lowers slide on bushings, usually two in each leg.

5 DROPOUTS

This is where the wheel is secured. The dropouts can be either open-ended for a quick release or closed for a through axle, either 15 or 20mm in diameter.

6 AIR VALVE

The majority of forks use an air spring. Adjusting the fork for your weight and riding style is a question of setting the correct air pressure via a Schrader valve. Some forks have positive and negative air chambers with a second valve at the bottom of the leg.

7 DAMPING ADJUSTERS

All but the cheapest forks have adjustable rebound damping, controlling how quickly the fork extends after a bump. Some also have adjustable compression damping, and a lockout lever to prevent the fork moving on smooth trails or roads is also common.

FRONT FORK SET-UP

Nearly every mountain bike has a suspension fork. There are plenty of fully rigid bikes out there if you want one, but you have to seek them out. While a suspension fork has substantial benefits for most riders, if you don't set it up correctly it'll be a liability.

1 Most forks have an O-ring on one of the stanchions that shows how much the fork has compressed. If there isn't one, wrap a small zip tie around the stanchion. Push the O-ring or zip tie down until it touches the fork wiper seal. If your fork has a lock-out lever, make sure it's disengaged.

2 Prop yourself up against a wall with your elbow, or ask for help to hold the bike upright, and sit on the bike in the normal riding position with your usual riding kit (including a pack if you normally ride with one). If you've compressed the fork a lot when getting on the bike, you will need to reach down and reset the O-ring. You are looking to spread your weight without bouncing on the saddle or pedals.

3 Being careful not to compress the fork further, climb off the bike and measure the sag directly from the fork leg. Sag should be between a quarter and a third of the total travel available. For example, on a 120mm fork you should look for sag of 30-40mm.

FACTORY SETTINGS

All forks have recommended settings for different rider weights. These can be found in the fork manual or in some cases handily on the fork itself. They usually give a range of pressures. The middle of the suggested range is a sensible starting point – use the setup procedure above to fine-tune from there.

4 If you have air-sprung forks there'll be an air valve on them somewhere – on RockShox and Fox forks it's on top of the left-hand leg. Remove the threaded cap to access the valve. If you have a coil-sprung fork, you should find a preload dial in the same place.

5 Use a shock pump to adjust the air pressure in the fork. If the fork has too much sag, add air. If it doesn't sag enough, let air out using the release valve on the pump. Make adjustments 5psi at a time then repeat steps 1-3. If you have a coil fork, turn the preload dial anticlockwise for more sag, clockwise for less sag.

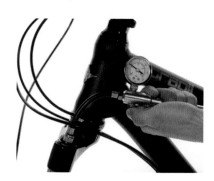

COIL SPRING REPLACEMENT

Coil forks are fitted with springs designed for a rider of average weight. If you're unusually light or heavy the available preload adjustment may not be sufficient. If you need the preload adjustment at one extreme or the other but the fork is still too soft or too hard, you'll need to change the spring(s). Usually this is a simple matter of removing the fork top caps, removing the existing spring and dropping in the replacement one. Be sure to get the right spring for your fork – sourcing replacements can be tricky for budget forks, though.

6 Some forks have a separate 'negative spring' that balances the main spring at rest for better performance on small bumps.

Set this to the same pressure as the main spring – you can adjust it a little either way to suit your preferred feel.

DAMPING ADJUSTMENTS

Most forks (except very cheap units) have some form of adjustable damping. The most common adjustment is rebound damping, which controls how quickly the fork returns to its rest position after hitting a bump. As a very rough rule of thumb, push hard and quickly down on the bars with flat hands and then lift your hands up as quickly as possible. The bars should keep pace with your hands – adjust the rebound damping to suit.

REAR SHOCK ANATOMY

1 BUSHINGS

All suspension designs require the shock to move slightly, so the mounting eyes are lined with bushings. These eventually wear and require replacement to avoid distracting clonking.

2 AIR CAN

Like forks, most shocks use an air spring, although you'll find steel coil springs on freeride and downhill bikes. The volume of the air can affects how the shock behaves as it compresses – a small air can makes the suspension harder the further it moves.

3 SHOCK SHAFT

The equivalent of the stanchions on a fork, the shaft is the fixed part over which the air can moves. Any damage or wear to the shaft can cause air leaks.

4 WIPER SEAL

The wiper seal works in the same way as those on forks. The difference is that it's a single, large seal. Behind it are O-rings to maintain air pressure, which is typically a lot higher than found in a fork.

5 AIR VALVE

Just as on a fork, shock adjustment is achieved by altering air pressure. The valve is a standard Schrader (car-type) valve, although you'll need a special shock pump to accurately adjust the pressure.

6 PROPEDAL LEVER

Fox shocks have a switchable damping circuit that resists movement caused by pedalling. It's activated by a lever on the shock body, with high-end shocks also having an adjustment dial to control the strength of the resistance. Other shock makers have similar systems.

7 REBOUND ADJUSTER

Nearly every shock has adjustable rebound damping to control how quickly the rear suspension extends after a bump. Getting this adjusted correctly is key to suspension performance.

REAR SHOCK SET-UP

AIR-SPRUNG SHOCK

Air-sprung shocks are now the most common type. As well as being lighter than coil-sprung shocks, they're also more adjustable, simply by adding or removing air. Air shocks can deal with riders across a very wide range of weights.

1 Before starting the setup process, make sure any lockout levers or platform damping adjusters are off or at the minimum setting. You need to have only the air spring supporting your weight.

2 Push the shock O-ring up the shock body so that it butts up against the air canister. The O-ring will be forced along the shock as it compresses, showing you how much travel you've used.

3 Propping yourself up against a wall with your elbow, sit on the bike in your normal riding position and usual riding kit (including pack if you use one). You'll probably need to reset the O-ring once the shock has settled.

4 Being careful not to compress the shock further, climb off the bike and measure the sag directly from the shock body. Some shocks, like the RockShox unit pictured, have a sag scale etched onto the shaft so you won't need a tape measure.

5 In general, you're looking for 25-35% of the available travel as sag. As an example, if your shock has 50mm of stroke you're aiming for about 12-17mm of sag. The ideal settings vary with different rear suspension designs, so consult your owner's manual – there's usually a suggested measurement there.

6 Use a shock pump to add or remove air until you've got the suggested sag setting. A higher pressure gives less sag, a lower air pressure gives more sag. Shock pumps have a pressure gauge – make a note of the correct pressure when you've got the sag right.

COIL-SPRUNG SHOCK

Coil-sprung shocks use a steel coil spring to support the rider's weight. This is heavier than a can of air, but for heavy-duty applications like freeride and downhill, coil springs have benefits. With no air seals, they're inherently reliable and there's no seal drag to hinder the action. Unlike an air-sprung shock, a coil spring is not a 'one size fits all' affair. The preload adjuster allows a small degree of tuning, but the best performance is achieved when the spring weight offers the correct amount of sag with minimal preloading – typically two turns of the preload collar. If you need more than that, a replacement spring will be needed.

1 Wind off all damping adjusters to their minimum setting. This is especially important for compression or platform damping, either of which will tend to hold the shock up and mask the effects of spring tuning.

2 To establish a starting point, unscrew the preload collar away from the spring to the point just before the spring starts to rattle with no weight on the saddle. Then wind it back two full turns.

3 The stiffness of a spring is called the spring rate, measured in pounds per inch – a 450lb spring will take a force of 450lb to compress 1 inch. Remember that the rear suspension acts as a lever – five inches of movement at the axle may be just two inches at the shock, which is why the spring needs to be stiffer than you might think.

4 Measure the unweighted eye-to-eye distance of the shock (between the mounting bolts). Next, sit on the saddle in normal riding gear and measure the weighted eye-to-eye distance – you may need a helper. Subtracting the second measurement from the first will tell you how much the shock has compressed.

5 Typically, sag should measure one quarter to one third of the entire shock stroke. Add preload to reduce sag, unwind preload for more sag. If you have too much sag with two or three turns preload you'll need a heavier spring, if you can't get enough sag even with no preload you'll need a lighter spring.

SWAPPING COIL SPRINGS

To change a coil spring it's easiest to remove the shock first (see page 160). With the shock off the bike, unwind the preload ring as far as it will go. This will let you move the spring far enough to remove the spring seat plate at the end of the shock – it's slotted so will slide off the shaft. Drop the spring off the end of the shock, put the new one on, replace the seat plate and refit to the bike.

ADJUSTING THE REBOUND DAMPING

With the sag set, the next step to achieving the perfect suspension set-up is to tune the damping. While air and coil springs suspend the rider, it's the oils and valves inside the shock that control the energy released by the spring. The most common available adjustment is rebound damping, which controls how fast the shock or fork returns (rebounds) to the sag position. Too much damping and the suspension will return slowly and won't be ready for the next hit; not enough damping causes the suspension to spring back uncontrollably.

Shocks and forks have a massive range of adjustment so it is very easy to get the rebound setting wrong. And because the majority of weight on a full suspension bike is supported by the rear suspension, it is the most important thing to get right. Before adjusting the damping, follow the steps outlined on pages 150-155 for setting the correct amount of sag. With the sag sorted and the rebound adjuster fully out, ride along a flat road or trail and give the rear suspension a firm 'pump' with your feet. The shock should return to the sag

position within two cycles – initial compression, rebound, slight compression, slight rebound, settle. If it bounces more than that, add more rebound damping. If it simply rebounds slowly back to the sag position, dial some damping out. This test will also help you to get the balance between front and rear damping correct. The two ends of the bike ideally need to rebound at the same speed to avoid pitching on the trail.

Fine tuning is best done on proper trails. If the bike feels too bouncy and skittish – most noticeable over larger drops or repeated bumps – you'll need more damping. If the suspension tends to 'pack down' over repeated bumps because it doesn't have time to return to the rest position before the next bump comes along, you'll need less damping.

OTHER DAMPING ADJUSTMENTS

More sophisticated shocks and forks will offer more adjustments. These let you really fine-tune the suspension to your preferences, although you'll need to build up a fair bit of riding experience before you've decided what those preferences are. Most beginner to intermediate riders are best

served by suspension units with simple spring and rebound damping adjustments.

Compression damping is the most common additional setting. This acts to slow the compression stroke but without affecting the sag. The most useful compression damping adjustment is for 'low speed' compression damping. Low speed here refers to the speed at which the suspension is compressing, not the speed at which the bike is moving. Typical examples include the tendency of a fork to compress under braking, or for suspension to bob when pedalling hard. Both of these can be countered with a little extra damping – the ProPedal lever found on many Fox shocks is essentially a low-speed compression control. Some forks and shocks offer a separate high-speed compression adjuster, which affects the behaviour of the fork over fast successions of smaller bumps.

You may also encounter various other systems designed to reduce the effect of pedalling action on the suspension. These include 'platform' dampers and inertia valves. These all have their own nuances and it's best to refer to the manufacturer's documentation for set-up information.

SAG AND FRAME GEOMETRY

The amount of sag you run affects the geometry of the bike. Slightly less sag in the rear shock will raise the bottom bracket and steepen the head angle, while more sag will lead to a lower bottom bracket and slacker head angle. Most bikes will work well across a range of sag settings, so you can choose anywhere in the stated range. Some bikes can be quite picky about sag, though, with a narrow range of numbers that work.

If you're riding steep, technical terrain where the switchbacks drop away suddenly, you may want to increase the spring rate in the fork. This reduces the amount of sag so that you ride higher in the travel. Not only will this slacken the head angle slightly, making the bike more stable at speed, but it will also stop the fork from diving as much, making those slow, tight, rocky switchbacks all the easier to clean. The downside is less absorption of smaller bumps – again, it's personal preference.

SHOCK STROKE

The stroke of your shock can usually be found either in the manufacturer's instructions or the specifications in the catalogue or website. If you don't know what it is, measure the amount of exposed shaft with the suspension fully extended, then deflate the shock completely, fully compress it and measure again. In most cases the shock will compress the whole length of the exposed shaft less than a millimetre or so, but some shocks have quite a bit of shaft still showing when fully compressed, so don't rely on that when calculating sag.

CARE AND REGULAR CHECKS FOR FORKS

Most riders neglect their forks, but the suspension is a moving part that is exposed to the elements so regular cleaning and lubrication are essential. Just like the drivetrain, neglect will cause premature wear and diminished performance, often resulting in irreparable damage. Internal servicing of forks is best carried out by experienced technicians – trying to strip forks without instructions and a set of sophisticated tools is asking for trouble. Essential cleaning and lubrication is straightforward, though. After every ride clean the stanchions and wiper seals, paying particular attention to the area between the fork brace and the seal. Add a drop of oil and massage it in by pumping the forks a few times. We're looking at a Fox fork here, but the basic arrangement is common to most forks.

STORAGE

If your bike is parked for a long time, the oil that lubricates the bushings tends to settle to the bottom of the fork, leaving the bushings dry. You may experience a slightly sticky fork action until the oil has recirculated. If you store your bike hanging by its front wheel, the oil will tend to stay in the bushings.

TOOLS REQUIRED

- Small flat-blade screwdriver
- Large flat-blade screwdriver
- Fox suspension fluid
- Clean rags

1 Cover the tip of a small flat-blade screwdriver with tape and wrap clean rags around the stanchions to protect the forks – you don't want to be scratching them. Use the screwdriver to pry the seals gently from the lower legs of the fork. The fork seals have small notches to make this easier.

2 Once the seals are loose, remove the rags and slide the seals all the way up to the crown. Take the same rags and wrap them around the junction of the upper and lower legs to stop dirt getting into the fork.

Use another rag to clean the outside edge of the seals. Remove all the dirt and inspect the seals for damage like cracks or scratches in the surface.

3 With the seals clean, turn your attention to the tops of the fork legs. Clean out any dirt that's found its way in under the seals, taking care not to damage the stanchions.

4 There are foam O-rings under the main seals, designed to hold some oil that gets transferred to the stanchions. Make sure that they're clean and undamaged.

5 If the foam O-rings are dry, use a few drops of suspension fluid to soak them. Then wipe the upper tubes clean and slide the seals back down onto the lower legs.

6 Press the seals fully home using a large, covered flatblade screwdriver, starting between the fork brace and the stanchions and working your way around to the back of the fork. Take care not to damage the seals. Cycle the fork a few times to make sure they're properly located.

FORK TROUBLESHOOTING

The fork is rocking
Check that the headset is tight (see pages 166-170). If the headset is fine, the fork bushings may be worn. Have the fork inspected by a professional suspension-tuning centre.

The fork is topping out
Increase the rebound damping. If the adjusters have no effect, you may have lost oil from the damper or it may be damaged internally.

The fork is bottoming out
The spring rate may be too soft, or there may be insufficient compression damping. If the sag is correct then you need to increase the damping. If an air-sprung fork won't hold air, professional servicing will be required.

The fork feels harsh
The spring could be too firm, or you may have too much compression damping resulting in a 'spike'. If the fork doesn't have an external compression adjuster, try using a lighter-weight oil in the fork.

The fork rebounds too quickly
Increase the rebound damping and, if the fork doesn't have an external rebound adjuster, try using a lighter-weight oil in the fork, assuming that the fork isn't friction damped.

After compression the fork takes ages to return to the sag position.
Completely back off the rebound damping and, if that doesn't cure the problem, get it checked out at an authorised service centre.

The fork action is notchy
This is probably due to stiction (static friction). Strip and clean the fork as per the manufacturer's instructions, or have it serviced at a recognised service centre.

REAR SHOCK MAINTENANCE

If you've got a full suspension bike, it doesn't take long to figure out that with all those moving parts something is bound to wear out. Invariably, the first thing to go is the DU bushing – that's the small collar in either end of the shock. Virtually all rear shocks, regardless of whether or not they are air- or coil-sprung, are fixed to the frame using DU bushings and aluminium fitting hardware. The bushings – and, in most cases, parts of the hardware – are designed to be perishable so that the inexpensive bushing wears, rather than expensive shock unit.

Shock and rider location both determine how quickly the bushing will wear out. On the whole, the bushings on shocks that are positioned in front of the seat tube last longer, as they are not in the firing line of mud being flung off the rear wheel. Also, if you live in a dry, dusty climate, chances are that the bushings could last for years.

Check shock bushings by gently lifting and pushing up and down on the saddle while keeping the rear wheel on the ground. Any clicking, knocking or loose sensations may point to worn bushings. Repeat with your fingers on each end of the shock where it mounts to the frame. Any movement will be easily detectable.

TOOLS REQUIRED

- Allen keys
- 10mm spanner
- Small sockets
- DU bushing tool

REPLACING A WORN BUSHING

1 Having identified which bushing is worn, you'll need to remove the shock. Shock mounting hardware varies between bikes, but usually you'll need either two Allen keys or one Allen key and a small socket to undo them.

WARNING

Do not attempt to dismantle shock units at home, as most shocks are charged with gas and dismantling them could result in serious injury. Always have your shock serviced at an authorised service centre. And, as always: read the manual!

2 This bike has a threaded shaft that passes through the frame and shock, with a bolt to secure it. The shaft is likely to be a snug fit and may need drifting out with a suitable tool. Usually threading the bolt back in a little way and gently tapping the end of it is sufficient.

3 Repeat at the opposite end and remove the shock completely. Supporting the rear wheel will take some load off the bolts and shafts and make them easier to remove. Watch out for the wheel dropping further than normal with the shock out.

REAR SHOCK TROUBLESHOOTING

The shock is losing air
Check that the valve body is tight in the air canister and that the valve core is also tight.

The shock is topping out
Increase the amount of rebound damping. If the shock still tops out, take it to an authorised dealer for inspection.

There is an excessive amount of oil on the shock shaft (coil) or body (air)
Clean and inspect the seal. If the leaking persists, the shock will need servicing.

My shock is making slurping noises
The oil has become emulsified, that is gas and oil are mixed together, which will result in inconsistent damping. Return the shock for a service.

The shock is stuck down
Usually this means that air has leaked to the wrong side of the main air chamber seal. You can try releasing the remaining air, cycling the shock and reinflating, but it's most likely to require professional attention.

4 If the DU bushing is worn, you should have no problem removing the alloy shock spacers by hand. These mounts are usually different from one end of the shock to the other, so note which end they came from. They're also specific sizes for different bikes and shocks.

5 If the alloy spacers don't come out easily, clamp them in the soft jaws of a vice and wiggle them out. Replacement bushing kits usually include the spacers as both items tend to wear together, so don't worry about damaging the old hardware.

6 With the spacers removed, it's time to tackle the DU bushing itself. This is a press fit in the shock body. It's possible to remove them with improvised tools, but the proper tool is easiest. Slide the thin end of the male portion of the bushing tool through the shock eyelet and slide the female portion on with the tapered end inwards.

7 Place both ends of the tool in a vice and slowly compress. The tapered part of the tool will push the bushing sideways until it pops out. If it doesn't move, check that the tool is assembled correctly.

8 Place a fresh bushing onto the thin end of the male tool and flip the female portion of the tool over so that the tapered end is outwards. Compress in a vice as before until the new bushing is flush with the face of the shock eye.

9 Fit the new shock spacers, making sure that they're in the right end. They'll be a tighter fit than the old, worn, spacers but should still push in by hand.

10 Re-install the shock. The spacers should be a snug fit between the mounting plates on the frame and swingarm. You'll need to lift the rear wheel to get the mounting holes to line up.

SHOCK TIPS

- When unbolting the shock, support the frame (or the rear wheel if the bike is in a stand) to stop the bike collapsing or overextending as this could damage the shock or frame. An old toe strap is good for this.

- Fit small O-rings between the DU bushings and fitting hardware to reduce dirt build-up. If you grease the bushing, wipe away any excess grease as it will retain dirt and accelerate wear. Have your shock serviced annually to maximise performance and longevity.

12

FRAME AND FORKS

The frame has always been the heart of the bike, the vital chassis upon which all the other parts depend. This is as true as ever, but nowadays the fork is at least as important. As suspension forks have become more capable and sophisticated, so they've had more influence on the ride of the bike as a whole. It's not uncommon for forks to be considerably more expensive than the frame to which they're attached, and forks tend to get swapped onto new frames rather than the other way around.

Assembling a complete bike from parts is often the ambition of the aspiring home mechanic, and it's well worth doing – there's no better way to get to know how things go together than to put them together yourself. If you fitted all the parts yourself, you're much better equipped to notice, diagnose and repair any problems. This is especially true of headsets, which are simple components but rely on the correct arrangement of hidden parts to work correctly.

Don't expect to save money by putting together your own bike – large manufacturers can buy components a lot more cheaply than you can. The advantages are in the knowledge gained, getting exactly the bike you want and of course the satisfaction of doing it yourself.

Even if you're not planning to build a bike from scratch, many of the procedures for frame preparation are useful for regular maintenance and for checking over the frame after a crash.

FORKS AND HEADSET

All but the very cheapest mountain bikes now come with threadless headsets. The first threadless headset to see widespread use was the Aheadset, with the word becoming the de facto generic term for threadless headsets during the time that they co-existed with the traditional threaded headset. Now that threadless headsets are all but ubiquitous, we'll refer to them simply as 'headsets'.

The headset is a very simple component and the unit is therefore easy to service. The system consists of two bearing races positioned at either end of the head tube. The races run in these bearings and are trapped by the fork at one end and the stem at the other. The stem clamps the system together and prevents it from coming loose. A well-prepared head tube and a properly fitted headset will help the unit last longer. Even the cheaper headsets on the market can last a long time if your bike is properly prepared and the unit is serviced regularly.

AHEADSET PARTS

Although simple in concept, headsets do have quite a number of parts that must all be assembled in the correct order and in the right orientation. The details vary between different headsets, but this is a typical unit.

1 **Crown race**
2 **Bottom cup (and bearing)**
3 **Top cup (and bearing)**
4 **Top race**
5 **Fork washer**
6 **Star-fangled nut**
7 **Top cap**
8 **Top cap bolt**

① ② ③ ④ ⑤ ⑥ ⑦ ⑧

TYPES OF HEADSET

Headsets are available in various sizes, with the stated size usually referring to the diameter of the fork's steerer tube. 1in threaded headsets crossed over from road bikes and were the standard fitment on early mountain bikes. In the early 1990s two bigger standards appeared, using 1 1/8in (OS, for 'oversized') or 1 1/4in ('Evolution') steerers. 1 1/8in became the dominant

standard, with the main change in the following years being an almost wholesale switch to threadless headsets.

In recent years there's been an explosion in headset standards. 1.5in steerers appeared on freeride bikes but never caught on in a big way. Semi-integrated (sometimes known as 'zero-stack') headsets use bearing cups that are pressed into a large-diameter head tube such that the bearings sit flush with

the ends of the tube rather than sitting outside them.

The first semi-integrated headsets had the same size bearing top and bottom and worked with the same forks as conventional headsets. Many bikes now come with forks with tapered steerers that use larger bearings at the bottom (where most of the loads are taken) and smaller ones at the top. The most common arrangement is a tube that tapers from 1 1/8in at the top to 1.5in at the bottom, although some manufacturers use 1 1/4in at the top.

Tapered systems have few downsides on carbon fibre or aluminium bikes, where the extra material needed in the frame doesn't add much weight. Adding metal to a steel frame, though, can have a significant impact, while manufacturing tapered head tubes can be challenging for custom builders. This resulted in the X44 headset, which uses a straight headtube with a 44mm internal diameter that accepts a semi-integrated top cup and external bottom cup to accommodate a 1 1/8in – 1 1/4in steerer tube.

You may also encounter other variations, like combining an X44-style external bottom cup with a conventional external top cup. This proliferation of standards has resulted in manufacturers like Hope and Cane Creek adopting a mix-and-match approach to headsets. Rather than buying a complete headset, you buy the top and bottom cups and bearings separately. This makes things easier for shops (which would otherwise have to keep stocks of all sorts of weird and wonderful headsets) and means that you're more likely to be able to get the right sizes.

Regardless of the dimensions of the bearings and shape of the steerer tube, all headsets go together in essentially the same way and have common adjustment and maintenance procedures.

TAPERED STEERER

X44 HEADSET

BASIC HEADSET ADJUSTMENT

1 To check the headset, apply the front brake and rock the bike backwards and forwards. You will feel or hear a slight knocking if the unit is loose. If you're not sure, rest your hand across the fork crown and bottom headset cup to feel any movement directly. Sometimes worn suspension fork bushings can knock too, but you can isolate the headset bearings by performing the test with the wheel turned 90°.

2 Undo the (usually two) bolts on the side of the stem. These bolts clamp the stem to the top of the steerer tube. As well as connecting the stem to the steerer so that you can steer, fixing the stem maintains the correct preload on the headset bearings.

3 Once you have loosened the clamp bolts, tighten the top cap slightly to take up any play in the system. You will only need a small nip to tighten the unit (to around 3Nm). If the headset has sealed cartridge bearings you'll be able to feel when the headset is tight. With loose bearings it's a little harder – be careful not to over-tighten the top cap.

4 If the top cap bolt becomes hard to turn but the headset is still loose, it's possible that the top cap has bottomed out on the fork steerer. The top of the steerer needs to be 2-3mm below the top of the stem to work properly. If the steerer is flush with the stem, add an extra thin spacer – it can go on top of the stem to leave the bar height unchanged.

STACK HEIGHT

If you're replacing a conventional external headset, you may need to pay attention to the stack height of the replacement. Stack height is the amount of space that the cups take up on the steerer (A + B).

If you are fitting a new headset, make sure that you buy a similar make or one with the same stack height, especially if you have few or no spacers between headset and stem. If the stack is too high, the stem won't have enough steerer to hold on to. Remember that most forks will be ruined if you cut the steerer too short as they can't be replaced easily, so always double-check your measurements before you cut.

HEADSET MAINTENANCE

1 Before removing anything, secure the fork to the frame with a toe strap or zip tie. When the stem and top cap are removed, only friction in the bearings will hold the fork into the frame and it's likely to fall out without anything else to stop it. This could damage the fork, or your foot.

2 Unbolt the front brake calliper from the fork. The front brake hose links the fork and bars, so you need to remove the calliper to be able to completely detach the fork. Loop the hose around the bars to keep it out of the way.

TOOLS REQUIRED

- **Allen keys**
- **Grease**

3 It's a good idea to prepare a clean surface to lay all the headset parts on as they come off to avoid confusion. Undo the top cap bolt and remove cap, bolt and any spacers above the stem. At this point the fork is still held in by the stem.

4 Loosen the stem clamp bolts and slide the stem and bars off the steerer. It's fine to let the bars hang from the frame by the gear cables and brake hoses, although you might want to protect the frame with a rag.

5 Lift off the upper bearing cover. There will be a tapered washer helping to hold this in place which can get stuck. Loosen or remove the toe strap and give the steerer a tap with a rubber mallet. If that doesn't work, give it a tap back up. Alternate down and up taps until the washer comes free.

6 You should now be able to slide the fork out of the frame, leaving the upper bearing sat in its cup. The lower bearing will either stay in its cup or come out on the fork steerer.

7 The bearings will be either a sealed cartridge or loose ball bearings, as shown here. Which you have makes little difference in use, but loose bearings can be cleaned and re-greased while cartridge bearings are easier to simply replace if necessary. Take everything out and clean it up either way.

8 Cartridge bearings can simply be removed and replaced if necessary, with a light smear of grease on the outside of the housing to stop them getting stuck in the cups.

9 Refit the forks, making sure that all the bearings, seals, covers, washers and spacers are in the right order. Tapered systems make this slightly easier because it's impossible to get the bearings in the wrong cups. Preload the bearings using the top cap.

10 Most stems have two clamp bolts, one on either side, so that the stem will not be pulled over to one side as you tighten the bolts. Do not over-or under-tighten these bolts. Retighten the stem clamp bolts to the recommended torque setting – 10–12Nm per bolt is adequate and will mean that the bars will still twist in the event of a crash.

11 Check that the bars are straight by lining the bars up with the front hub. Slightly loosen the stem clamp bolts and twist the stem straight if necessary. Refit the front brake. Finally, check that the headset is adjusted properly and correct if needed.

REPLACING A HEADSET

To install a headset correctly, you need some specialist tools that you may not consider worth owning for occasional use. If you're replacing a headset the frame should already be correctly prepared, but this isn't always the case for new frames. Preparation requires even more specialist tools and is generally best left to a bike shop – we include the instructions here just in case. Titanium and carbon frames are usually prepared in the factory, aluminium and steel ones may need attention. We're combining fork and headset fitting here – ignore the redundant steps if you're fitting a new fork to an existing headset or a new headset without a new fork.

1 Remove the fork (see page 169). Old headset cups can be removed with a cup-removing tool like this one,

TOOLS REQUIRED

- **Allen keys**
- **Cup-removing tool**
- **Mallet**
- **Crown race removing tool**
- **Headset press tool**

which splays out inside the head tube and ensures a snug fit on the inside of the cups. Using a long screwdriver is not advisable as it can damage the inside of the frame and ruin the cups.

2 Tap the cup-removing tool with a mallet to remove the cups. With some smaller head tubes it can be tricky to get the tool to fit properly, as the jaws can be restricted by the other race. Be careful and make sure you wrap a cloth around the cup to prevent it pinging off around the workshop.

3 Remove the old crown race from the fork. The crown race is a very tight fit and really needs a crown race tool to remove. They can be shifted with a soft drift and a mallet, but the proper tool is much safer.

4 This dual-purpose cutter faces the head tube and also cuts the inside of the tube at the same time, making sure that the headset cups are inserted squarely into the tube. The top and the bottom of the tube are faced to ensure that the cups are parallel, so they don't work against each other and wear out quickly. It will remove any rust or paint on the tube and make sure the cups are a perfect fit.

5 A properly faced head tube will look perfectly flat and shiny. Clean out all the swarf from the inside and grease the top and bottom faces with some anti-seize grease. Grease the inner parts of the cups too, and check to see which is the top and which is the bottom (the logos are usually a dead giveaway).

6 It's possible to fit headset cups with improvised tools, but a proper headset press will do the job in seconds and will prevent any damage to the frame or headset components. Insert the cup so that it is straight and cannot distort as you force it in with the tool. There are usually chamfered edges on the cups to get them started. Line up the logos too so the front end looks tidy.

7 The same tool is used to fit semi-integrated headset cups – make sure you choose the correct die to fit your headset. The tool has a variety of dies that fit different sized cups. Make sure that you use one that fits well but not too snugly as the force on the tool can seize onto the aluminium cup and ruin it. Inspect the cups closely to check that they are flush with the tube – hold the bike up to the light and see if there are any gaps.

8 Fit the new crown race to the fork. This tool is used to knock the crown race onto the crown – make sure that the adaptor is a good fit to

the race and remove any rubber or plastic seals before you do this as they can be damaged. If you don't have a crown race tool, consider buying a cartridge bearing headset with a split race. This is a good idea for suspension forks with large crowns, which present problems when trying to remove the race.

9 Assemble the headset, making sure that all the seals, bearings, caps, washers and spacers are the right way up and in the correct order. The headset should all push together snugly, if there are any gaps it's likely that something's in the wrong place or incorrectly oriented.

10 Fit the front brake calliper, adjust the headset and tighten the stem clamp bolts as described on page 170. Sometimes a new headset beds in slightly during the first few miles of riding, so check the adjustment frequently until it settles down.

FITTING A FORK

1 Start by removing the old fork and removing the fork crown race as described in the previous sections. If you're replacing the headset too, do that first. If you're using the existing headset then measure the length of the old fork steerer from the crown to the top and transfer that to the new one. Mark the steerer with a permanent marker pen. Do not scratch a mark with a file or hacksaw blade as it could be wrong and the scratch will act as a stress riser and weaken the steerer. Fit the crown race to the new fork (see left).

2 Assemble the complete system at this point to check you have the steerer at the right length. Although you may not want to cut the steerer twice, it's better to allow for more spacers if you are unsure how high you want your bars. If in doubt, allow

TOOLS REQUIRED

- **Sharp hacksaw**
- **Fork cutting guide**
- **Star-fangled setting tool**
- **Permanent marker pen and ruler**
- **Allen keys**
- **Metal half-round file**
- **Mallet**
- **Crown race removing tool**

an extra 30mm for spacers. There's no problem in running spacers above the stem for a while until you've settled on a bar height.

3 Cut the steerer to length using a sharp new hacksaw blade, holding the steerer in a cutting guide to stop the blade wandering as you cut. If you don't have a cutting guide, an old stem can be used as a guide. It is essential that the cut is square to ensure that the stem fits properly and the star nut can be installed easily. If you are cutting a carbon fibre steerer, wear a facemask and use a fine blade.

4 File off any burrs on the outside and inside of the steerer tube with a half-round file. Take care not to scratch the steerer and make sure that the edges of the tube will not scratch the inside of the stem when you replace it. The inside has to be clear so that the top cap nut can be easily inserted inside the tube.

5 The star-fangled nut is the fixed part of the system and allows the top cap to fasten down on the headset stack, and also allows you to adjust out any play in the system. Use a nut setting tool and you can't fail to get it set straight in the steerer. Star-fangled nuts are only to be used on steel or aluminium steerers – carbon fibre steerers (rare on mountain bikes) need an expanding wedge instead.

6 Once inserted, the star-fangled nut is very hard to remove as they fit by wedging themselves into the inside of the tube. This scratches the tube, so removing the nut can make a big mess of both the nut and the steerer. If the star-fangled nut is damaged, simply knock it further down the steerer and fit a replaceable wedge.

7 Alternatively, you can use a cap and replaceable top wedge. These are safer and can be refitted, which is really important if you don't have a star-fangled nut setting tool. They also cannot damage the inside of the steerer tube and are essential for carbon steerers. You can also use a head lock, essentially a long bolt that extends all the way to a threaded plug in the bottom of the steerer.

8 Drop the lower bearing seal and bearing on to the crown race, grease as necessary and then insert the fork. Assemble the rest of the headset on the top of the steerer, fit the stem and top cap and adjust as described on page 168.

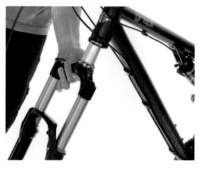

THE FRAME

FRAME CHECKS AND PREPARATION

Frame alignment is the first step to building your perfect bike. This is easier to ascertain on a hardtail than it is on a full suspension bike. The head tube and seat tube have to be in line in order for the bike to handle properly, and the rear dropouts have to be positioned so that they hold the rear wheel directly behind the front wheel. This is called frame track. Crashing can cause invisible damage to mountain bikes, so track should be regularly checked out. Use some of the following steps as they will help you identify problems and damage. This assessment is essential if you want to keep safe and prevent further accidents should components or frames fail.

1 The Park frame alignment tool used here makes alignment assessment easier. The tool rests on the head tube and seat tube, and the pointer gauge is adjusted to sit on the outside of the dropout. The gauge is then set and flipped over to the other side. If the bike is symmetrical, the gauge will not have to be re-adjusted.

TOOLS REQUIRED

- **M6 and M5 taps and tapping wrench**
- **Cutting paste**
- **Cleaning kit, including rags and degreaser/spray lube**
- **Frame alignment tool**
- **Rear dropout alignment tool**
- **Rear derailleur alignment tool**
- **String**
- **Ruler**
- **Vernier callipers**

2 Another simple way to check alignment is with a long piece of string. Wrap it around the head tube and trap either end under the quick-release skewer, or get someone to hold it, while you measure the string. The string needs to be very taut. We have removed the wheel for clarity but it should be in place for an accurate reading.

3 On a full suspension bike, it can be easier to use the string technique rather than the alignment gauge; the shock and pivots often stick out at the seat tube so there is no place for the alignment tool to rest. Interrupted seat tubes can also create problems. But whatever frame you have, the principle remains the same: the head and seat tubes must align with the rear dropouts.

4 The critical measurement will be between the seat tube and either side of the length of string. A difference of 1–2mm is acceptable and won't affect the bike's handling. However, if you have crashed and the measurement is more than 4–5mm, the frame may require attention from either a qualified frame builder or the manufacturer.

5 The dropout alignment tools shown here are used to check that the rear end is correctly spaced and aligned for the rear wheel. With the dropout tools fully inserted in the drop out, the central sections can be adjusted to meet in the middle. If they don't meet up, the dropouts have been twisted. These tools are long so that the mechanic can 'cold set' (bend) them slightly to meet perfectly.

7 Cantilever studs can also rust up. Tapping the threads will ensure that the bolts secure the brake firmly and that the bolt will not be cross-threaded as you tighten it. On good frames the studs are replaceable and it's worth replacing them every year or so as they do wear and make the brakes rattle around. If you have excessive brake squeal, new studs can be the solution.

9 The rear derailleur hanger is possibly the most vulnerable part of the mountain bike frame. Many frames have replaceable hangers, which may require replacing after a serious crash. Simply unbolt the replaceable part and order a new one from your dealer. Steel frames usually have non-replaceable hangers but they can be straightened. The rear derailleur alignment tool used here allows you to check and cold set the gear hanger.

6 Bottle-bolt bosses get bunged up with paint and, on steel frames, can rust up. Aluminium frames have riveted bottle bosses, which can be replaced with a specialist tool. Tap out the threads before you attach a bottle cage with an M5 tap. Be careful not to go too far. You will need the same size tool for rack fittings and cable guides as well, so it's worth buying one.

8 Disc brake mounts must be aligned correctly for proper brake function. Slight misalignment can be corrected with a facing tool like this Magura one. Brake mount alignment is less critical with post-mount brakes or adaptors but very important for IS mounts.

10 Once you have screwed the tool into the derailleur hanger, you can position it at several points around the wheel. The gauges on the tool allow you to lock it off using the wheel rim as a reference. If the gap between the gauges varies, you will have to adjust the dropout until there is a uniform gap all around.

11 Bottom bracket threads must be prepared before fitting the bottom bracket. This process cleans out any paint, rust and material from the shell and ensures that the threads are running parallel. Tap the threads using a quality in-line tap set. Remember that the drive-side or right crank is a left-hand thread (tightens anti-clockwise) and the non-drive-side or left crank is a right-hand thread (tightens clockwise). Double-check that you have the right cutters before you use them. Turn the cutters gradually and evenly – don't force them in, they should cut easily. Use plenty of cutting paste and keep turning until the cutters sit flush into the frame.

FRAME TIPS

- Rust is the first step on the road to steel frame failure. Corrosion shows that parts and frames are weakened, so clean off and treat rust as soon as it develops. On frames this can be best done by a re-spraying service.

- On steel frames use Waxoil on the inside of the frame tubes to protect them from rust. This is a spray-on treatment and helps prevent rust forming on the inside of your frame. This stuff is used on car chassis and tubes that are left outside.

- Get together with some riding buddies and all buy one expensive frame tool each. You can then share around the bigger workshop tools when you need them.

- Titanium doesn't rust. It's also really tough, so it will blunt taps and threading frame tools. Be careful when buying a titanium bike and make sure the frame comes pre-prepared – many bike shops will refuse to re-face and tap titanium bottom brackets as it blunts expensive cutters. If a titanium frame needs facing, take it to a specialist frame builder.

- Full suspension bikes need to be in track, but often any misalignment will be just pivot wear and tear. Replace pivot bushes regularly and check that the bolts are tightened to the recommended torque. Always follow the manufacturer's recommendations.

- Finally, remember to cover the frame at the points that rub on the cables and place a chainstay protector under the chain. These vulnerable positions will wear through the paint in no time, usually on the first ride. Neoprene protectors are a good idea as the chain literally bounces off them.

12 Once you have tapped the threads, you can face the outside edge of the bottom bracket. When you are using the facing tool, you will need plenty of cutting paste. Remember not to run the tool backwards as this can damage the cutter. Keep a close eye on the bracket face and check that it is clear of paint and completely square (it should look smooth and shiny all over).

13

ON THE TRAIL FIXES

Armed with the knowledge in the preceding chapters, you should be fully equipped to keep your bike in top condition. But no matter how meticulous your maintenance, there's always the possibility of something going wrong out on the trail. Vigilant checking and tuning will prevent a lot of failures, but it won't stop you crashing or getting a puncture. Self-sufficiency is part of mountain biking – if you're out in the wilds and something on your bike breaks, it's up to you to sort it out and get home.

Modern mountain bikes are very robust, so major failures are rare. In the early days bikes were somewhat fragile and magazines were full of tales of get-you-home repairs based on sticks, bits of string, rocks and other things you might find by the trail. These are mostly pretty ineffective, and with adequate preparation you should be able to tackle most things properly. You might not be able to restore 100% function, but if you can ride out that's good enough.

CHANGING A TUBE

Punctures are the single most common mechanical issue encountered during rides. We described how to patch a punctured inner tube in Chapter 10, but you don't want to be patching tubes by the side of the trail especially if it's wet or cold. If you get a puncture, it's best to change the tube and patch the old one at your leisure later on. You may also need to fit a tube on the trail even if you use tubeless tyres. Any hole too big for sealant to deal with will need a tube in to get you home.

1 As soon as you realise you have a flat, stop. It's better to get on with fixing the flat than trying to ride any further on a potentially hazardous wheel. Riding with a flat can also damage the rim should you hit anything hard on the trail and is likely to damage the tyre too. Stopping straight away may also allow you to find the hole in the tyre and remove any sharp objects that may have become trapped in the tread. Remove the wheel and either lay the bike down or hang it from a suitable branch. See page 118 for more on removing wheels.

TOOLS REQUIRED

- **Tyre levers**
- **Spare tube (or puncture kit)**
- **Mini-pump**

2 Most mountain bike tyres are quite loose fitting and it's usually possible to remove them without tyre levers, or with just one (although it's a good idea to carry two or three). Let any remaining air out of the tyre and remove the nut from the valve. Work around the tyre and push the bead inwards away from the rim walls. Starting opposite the valve, push the beads down into the well of the rim, working the resulting slack around the wheel. By the time you get round to the valve side there should be enough slack to pop the bead over the edge of the rim (see chapter 10 for fuller explanations).

3 If you can't get the tyre off without tyre levers (tubeless tyres can be a very tight fit), try using a single one first. Push the tyre away from the rim to reveal the bead, slip the lever tip under the bead and prise it over the edge of the rim. Then run the lever around the rim to remove one side of the tyre. If you can't pop enough bead over the rim with one lever, try two. Hook them both under the bead but lever with one first, then the other. The second lever will be harder to pull.

CLEAR THE TRAIL

When the inevitable happens and you have to stop by the trail to repair something, make sure that you leave the trail clear. Obstructing the trail with bits of bike is potentially dangerous. Get everything off to the side of the trail and ideally move to a section with good visibility.

4 Whichever method you use, there's no need to remove the tyre completely. You just need to pull one bead off the rim so you can remove the inner tube. Push the valve back up through the hole and pull the tube out from inside the tyre. Pack it away for repair later.

5 Then check the inside of the tyre for thorns or other pointy objects. Carefully run a gloved hand around the inside of the tyre – you'll be able to feel anything significant. Leaving the tyre on the rim can help you to find whatever caused the puncture. If you can find the hole in the tube and the tyre hasn't moved on the rim, you can use the position of the hole to track down the culprit. Use the position of the valve on the tube and the valve hole in the rim as a reference.

TRAIL TIPS

1   On very long rides, take some lube with you. Use it on your chain and derailleurs, especially if it's muddy or really dusty.

2   If you flat, take your time. Make sure you check several times for thorns in the tyre before you fix the tube or replace it.

3   Always repair and re-use tubes.

4   Carry a patch kit as well as spare tubes – you might run out of tubes.

5   Don't put a branch in your stem to use as a replacement handlebar – walk home or catch the bus if your bike is unrideable.

6   Stuffing your tyres with twigs and trail debris is an okay idea if home isn't too far away and you're on smooth terrain. And you have a sense of humour.

7   Take your rubbish and bits of broken bike home with you.

8   Remember to secure your tool kit so you don't scatter your favourite tools all over your favourite trail.

9   If you go on big adventure rides, take all the tools you would need to strip everything, and carry First Aid supplies.

10 Close gates, smile at farmers and don't race sheep – they're fast and unpredictable.

6 Self-adhesive patches are useful for trail repairs if you've run out of tubes, but they're not as effective as glued-on patches. If you find a large gash or split in the tyre (most likely to be in the sidewall) you'll need to use a tyre boot inside the tyre to stop the inner tube bulging out. Proper self-adhesive boots are available, but you can improvise with duct tape, cardboard or energy bar wrappers. Whatever you use is only a temporary fix – torn sidewalls mean a new tyre.

▶

7 Having identified and remedied the cause of the puncture, you're safe to fit a new inner tube. Slightly inflate the replacement tube with a couple of strokes of a mini-pump, just enough for the tube to take shape. Next, insert the valve into the valve hole. Make sure that the valve is seated properly into the rim, then push the tyre over the top of the tube. Work the tube carefully into the casing of the tyre.

8 Now, start to return the tyre bead into the rim. Start opposite the valve hole and work the tyre either side with two hands. Push the tyre beads right down into the well of the rim to produce enough slack to pull the last part of the tyre on by hand. This can be a bit of a struggle depending on the rim and tyre model. However, it is best to pull it on this way as using a tyre lever can pinch the tube as you lever it on.

9 Once the tyre is back on the rim, check that the beads are all in place and that the inner tube isn't pinched between tyre and rim. Pump the tyre up to the recommended pressure. If the tyre doesn't run true (it wobbles as you spin the wheel) re-seat it by letting most of the air out and pulling the tyre away from the bead. This will help the bead sit into the rim and usually 'pops' the tyre into place.

10 Refit the wheel in the bike, making sure that the quick-release skewer or through axle system is securely tightened. Give the wheel a spin to check that the brakes aren't rubbing. If they are, the wheel may not be in exactly straight.

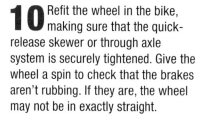

RIDING ALONE

Riding alone is inevitable. If you intend to ride all day, it's always better to ride with a group, but if it can't be avoided remember to tell someone where you are going and how long you'll be. You must remember to cover any breakdown eventuality and carry sufficient tools and spares to get you home. Take a mobile phone with you too, although you don't have to turn it on all the time if you want a peaceful ride. Some change for a payphone is a good backup plan.

TOP 10 TRAIL FAILS (and how to fix them)

1 PUNCTURES

Cause: A fact of life if you ride off-road. Thorns, sharp stones and other trail debris can all cause punctures.

Prevention: Run tyres at their recommended pressures. Check tyre treads for anything that could work through the tyre and cause a flat. Replace tyres regularly.

Trail fix: Carry spare tubes and a puncture kit. If you are really stuck, tie a tight knot in the tube on either side of the hole, which might get you home.

2 TYRE DISASTERS

Cause: Gashes from flints or stones, or the brake block rubbing on the tyre.

Prevention: Check tyres for wear and replace regularly. Run tyres at their recommended pressures.

Trail fix: Use a tyre boot to patch the inside of the tyre. You can also use big puncture patches and stiff cardboard.

3 BROKEN CHAIN

Cause: Twisting strain on links of the chain, usually in combination with a very worn or badly fitted chain.

Prevention: Use a quality chain, check for wear often and replace it regularly. Don't use gears with extreme crossovers (big ring to big sprocket) and ease pressure when shifting.

Trail fix: Carry a SRAM Powerlink, which will work with most chains.

4 BROKEN SPOKES

Cause: Usually uneven tension in the spokes, which normally happens when the wheel is reaching the end of its life.

Prevention: Regular checkups with a competent wheelbuilder, and having good wheels built in the first place with regular tension.

Trail fix: Folding 'cable spokes' are available, which can fold away into a tool kit.

5 RIM/WHEEL FAILURE

Cause: Crashes, poor build, loose spokes and big hits. Rims can wear through and the bead can detach from the rim, which can be catastrophic!

Prevention: Look for wear and dents in the rim and check spoke tension.

Trail fix: Wobbles can be rectified with a spoke key, bigger distortions can be pushed out with brute force, but only if a spoke key can't do the job.

6 GEAR CABLE FAILURE

Cause: Forcing the gear to shift, or simple wear and tear.

Prevention: Keep the cables lubricated and free-running. Replace cables (inners and outers) regularly.

Trail fix: The gear stops can be adjusted to run in a suitable single gear to get you home, or you can clamp the cable under a bottle boss bolt. Or carry a spare.

7 BRAKE CABLE OR HOSE FAILURE

Cause: Brake cables can fray and break and hydraulic hoses can be pulled out in a crash.

Prevention: Use quality cables and replace them regularly.

Trail fix: Carry spare cables, one for the brakes and one for the gears. There's not much you can do about a failed hydraulic hose, though. Ride carefully home with the remaining brake.

8 FREEWHEEL FAILURE

Cause: Broken pawls in the freehub/cassette body.

Prevention: Regular servicing and replacement, if necessary.

Trail fix: Secure the cassette to the spokes with zip ties and you can ride home with a crudely fixed gear.

9 REAR MECH FAILURE

Cause: The mech can get stuck in the spokes and break, or get damaged after a crash.

Prevention: Check that the rear mech is straight and correctly adjusted.

Trail fix: Remove the rear mech and go 'singlespeed'.

10 CHAIN STUCK

Cause: Either worn chainrings or chain. The chain can get trapped onto the chainring and jammed into the frame.

Prevention: Replace worn chainring and/or chain.

Trail fix: Try to use the big chainring to get home.

OTHER POTENTIAL PROBLEMS

THE CRANKS SNAP OR LOOSEN

Heavily used cranks may eventually break from fatigue – cracks usually appear first, so keep a close eye on them. Modern two-piece cranks are less prone to loosening off than square taper units, but it can still happen. Whatever the style of crank, don't carry on riding if they're loose – they'll be ruined quite quickly. Carry the correct size Allen key or spanner to fit the bolts.

THE PEDALS GET SMASHED OR FALL OFF

It is possible to ride with one foot, but it is a bit uncomfortable. If the pedal spindle is still intact you could try riding on that. Or wedge a suitably-sized stick in the pedal thread – don't expect it to take much weight, but it might be slightly better than nothing.

THE STEM SNAPS OR BENDS

This is rare, and there's not much you can do about it after it's happened. Don't attempt to ride a bent or cracked stem, and if you notice it failing during a ride then find some other way to get home. Munching the broken end of a stem is highly uncomfortable.

THE BARS SNAP OR BEND

You can get home using just one side of the bar if you shift it through the stem and just use one brake lever, but you won't be able to go far. Bent bars are just waiting to snap, so if you have a bad crash and they get bent replace them.

SEATPOST FAILURE

Seatpost breakages can be caused by fatigue or crashes. Check the post regularly with a straight edge – if it's bent, replace it. If your saddle comes off on a ride you'll have to ride out standing up.

THE HEADSET LOOSENS

Headsets can occasionally come loose, leading to a knocking sound and sensation from the front end. This should be tackled immediately to avoid damaging the beatings – threadless headsets usually just need a simple Allen key tweak (see page 168).

THE FRAME SNAPS

Time to walk home. Don't try to get creative with coat hangers or bracken, just plan your letter to the warranty department and call a taxi. Riding broken frames will be very dangerous, possibly fatal, so don't try it. Bent frames are just waiting to snap, so if your frame looks like it's bent get it checked out by a mechanic or frame builder.

BUCKLED WHEEL

If the buckle is incurable with a spoke key, try standing on it and get one of your riding mates to stand on the other side of the buckle. Then you can jump up and down on the other side. This is a last resort – the wheel may pop back into shape, but this will probably ruin the rim and the spokes.

FORK FAILURE

A broken fork usually leads to a sudden and severe crash. Inspect forks regularly for any cracks, bends or suspicious discolouring. Steerer tube failures tend to occur where the tube joins the crown. This area can only be inspected by removing the fork. Suspension forks can fail internally, either losing air pressure or damping. If the fork won't hold air you can use the lockout lever (if present) to hold it up. Loss of damping will mean a very bouncy fork that you can only ride slowly on, but it'll get you home.

BRAKE PAD FAILURE

With regular checking you shouldn't wear out brake pads mid-ride, but some combinations of soil type, weather conditions and pad compound don't mix happily. Many riders have been caught out by premature pad failure. Fortunately pads are small, easy to carry and easy to fit, so take a couple of spare sets with you just in case.

FULL SUSPENSION FAILURES

These depend very much on how severe the failure is. If the frame fails then it's very dangerous to ride it. If the shock fails you can usually ride home without too many problems, but you risk damaging the suspension unit or the frame so take it easy.

THE CHAINRING BENDS

The chainring can usually be bent back with some gentle persuasion (a big rock) or with a pair of pliers. A chainring tooth will break off quite easily, however, so don't force it.

TRANSPORTING YOUR BIKE

Most people don't have great riding from their doorstep, so it's likely that at some point you'll need to take your bike somewhere by car. There are several options for transporting your bike, each with advantages and disadvantages.

IN YOUR CAR

The safest way to carry your bike is in the back of your car. First, remove both the wheels (see pages 118-122). If you have hydraulic disc brakes, place a spacer between the pads just in case you activate the levers when placing your bike in the boot. Wrap the chain and rear derailleur in a cloth so as not to get oil all over the place.

Try to pack your bike last and on top of (or alongside if your car permits) all your other kit and lay the wheels under the frame. It's a good idea to get some wheel bags (bin liners are good too), especially if it's been muddy or wet. Try not to let the tyres rub on anything sharp or you'll have a nasty shock when the sidewalls wear a hole and puncture.

ON A ROOF RACK

Remove all loose-fitting equipment, such as drink bottles, tool packs, pumps and so on. There are various styles of roof rack, but whichever it is make sure all the clamps and straps are done up and give the bike a good shake to make sure it's secure. Before you drive off, double-check that all the straps are tight and you haven't left anything on the floor around the car or on top of the roof.

If you stop for anything, lock the bikes to the rack (most racks now have lockable fork fastenings) and always use a roof rack with lockable roof brackets. Lastly, don't go into a supermarket or height-limited car park as this will ruin your bike, car and roof rack. And yes, it does happen more often than you might think!

ON A REAR RACK

Racks that strap on to the boot lid are inexpensive and hence popular, but you have to be careful not to damage the car and they can be awkward to fit and load securely. You may also need to add a numberplate and lighting board if those on the car are obscured. The best type of boot rack is one that fits to a tow bar and supports the bikes by the wheels. We've fitted tow bars to cars just to be able to use such a rack. Most tow bars can take the weight of a rack and three bikes, and those on larger cars will take four. Just be aware that the rack sticks out behind the car quite a long way.

PACKING YOUR BIKE

If you're flying with a bike, you'll need to pack it safely and securely. We have successfully flown with unpacked bikes with just the bars turned, but most airlines insist on them being boxed or bagged. Hard cases offer the best protection in transit, but they're expensive and heavy. Padded bags are cheaper, lighter and less likely to incur excess baggage charges but you need to pack them carefully to ensure your bike arrives safe and sound. The cheapest option of all is a big cardboard box like the ones bikes are delivered to shops in. Shops usually have to pay to get rid of these, so you can usually get one for free if you ask nicely. Add plenty of bubble wrap and tape. Whichever method you choose, remove your pedals, saddle and seatpost first, wrap these up in a jiffy bag and place them straight into the bag, box or into your hand luggage – don't leave them on the kitchen table. We like to pack helmet, shoes and pedals (and maybe saddle) in our hand luggage just in case the bike ends up in the wrong place. At least then we can hire a bike and have familiar contact points.

1 Remove the wheels and take out the quick-release skewers. Even though luggage holds are pressurised, airlines still want tyres and suspension units to be deflated. Leave a little air in the tyres just to protect the rims and to provide some more padding. Place the wheels in the bag and tape them to one another, or use electrical zip ties. Space them so that the cassette and axle will not damage the frame. Cover the ends of the axle with cardboard to prevent them causing any damage inside the bag.

2 Remove the handlebars (whether or not you have to do this will depend on the type of bag you are using). If you are packing your bike in a bike box, you may well have to remove the bars to fold the bike flat. If you do, tighten the bolts that you have removed to prevent losing them and wrap the bars in bubble wrap. Tape anything like this in place with duct tape as it will damage your paintwork and ruin components if it rattles around.

3 Remove the rear mech. This is worth doing as it's vulnerable and is one less thing to be sticking out and risk getting bent as your bike is thrown into the hold. Wrap it up in a plastic bag along with the chain. Duct tape it to the rear triangle, safely out of the way.

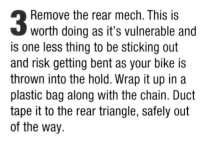

4 Use plenty of pipe lagging to protect the frame and around the suspension forks and the cranks too, as it absorbs a lot of shock. Lastly, don't forget to pack your pump, tools and, most importantly, a pedal spanner.

GLOSSARY

Items in italics denote another glossary entry.

29er: A bike with 29in wheels rather than the long-established 26in standard. Bigger wheels roll more easily over bumps, but add a little weight and can make bike fit awkward for shorter riders.

32 hole: The most common drilling for hubs and rims, to accommodate 32 spokes. In general, more spokes makes for a stronger wheel, although wheels with fewer than 32 spokes are increasingly popular. 36 hole components are also available, but for most purposes 32 spokes are ample.

4130: A grade of *chromoly* steel tubing, commonly used for frames. It's light, strong and easy to work with.

4X: A racing format involving four riders going head to head on a short downhill course characterised by berms, large jumps and a choice of lines.

6061 aluminium: Aluminium alloyed with magnesium and silicon. Light and easy to work, 6061 is commonly used for frames although it needs to be artificially aged and heat-treated after welding.

650B: Wheel size that sits between 26 and 29in. Rolls better than 26in but easier to package into full suspension or small hardtail frames than 29in.

7000-series aluminium: Any of various aluminium alloys with similar properties to 6061 but not requiring post-welding heat treatment for full strength.

Active suspension: Rear suspension designed to be unaffected by forces from pedalling or braking.

Adjustable cup: Cartridge-style bottom bracket units usually have one fixed cup that's permanently attached to the bearing sleeve, and one adjustable cup that's wound in to align the unit in the frame.

Aheadset: Trade name for Dia-Compe's original design of threadless headset, now often used as a generic term for all such headsets

Air spring: Suspension spring using compressed air. Lighter and easier to adjust than a coil spring, but needs more maintenance.

Anti-suck plate: Bolt-on frame fitting that prevents the chain from jamming between chainring and frame in the event of *chain suck*.

Bar end: Bolt-on handlebar extension that provides an alternative hand position for climbing.

Bottom bracket: The axle and bearing assembly on which the crankarms rotate. The part of the frame into which the bottom bracket fits is called the bottom bracket shell.

Bradawl: A pointed tool designed for making pilot holes for screws. Useful for opening out the ends of freshly-cut cable housing.

Braze-on: Any frame fitting, including those for mounting cables, bottle cages, racks and so on. Such fittings are only actually brazed on to steel frames, but they're still called that even if welded, glued or riveted in place.

Bushing: a rotating bearing without balls or rollers, often used in rear suspension pivots.

BSO: Bicycle-Shaped Object, derogatory term for very cheap, poorly-made bikes sold in supermarkets.

Butting: A process used on steel, titanium or aluminium tubes whereby the ends are drawn thicker for strength at stress or weld points. The middle section of the tubes can be made thinner and therefore lighter as they are under less stress. Spokes can also be butted to save weight.

Cable puller: A plier-like tool that pulls a brake cable tight while pushing against the brake arm, making cable adjustment a two-, rather than three-handed job.

Cassette: A stack of sprockets that slides onto a splined *freehub*. This design replaced the screw-on freewheel – by integrating the freewheel mechanism into the hub rather than the sprockets, the hub bearings can be placed further apart for strength. Cassette sprockets are also much easier to remove than threaded freewheels. Most modern MTBs now have 10-speed cassettes, although 9, 8 and 7 speed parts are still readily available.

Cantilever brake: Traditional *rim brake* design using two pivoting arms joined by a straddle cable. Lightweight, simple and reliable, but trickier to adjust than a V-brake.

Cartridge bearing: Self-contained, sealed unit comprising inner and outer races and ball bearings. Cartridge bearings are generally replaced rather than serviced.

Cassette lock ring: Threaded fitting used to secure a *cassette* to a *freehub*. Requires a specific splined tool to fit or remove.

Centre to centre: The measurement from the centre of the *bottom bracket* axle to the centre of the top tube along the seat tube, one of the ways of stating frame size. Centre to top is more commonly used, although many bikes now are simply described as small, medium, large etc.

Chain checker: Gauge to assess how worn a chain is. Worn chains lead to faster wear on sprockets and chainrings, so replacing them in good time can save a big parts bill.

Chainline: The alignment of the chainrings and rear sprockets. The ideal chainline puts the middle chainring exactly in line with the centre of the cassette, although the current standard MTB chainline puts the chainrings slightly further out to accommodate large frame tubes.

Chainline gauge: Tool for checking *chainline*.

Chain slap: The annoying sound of the chain tap-dancing on your chainstay paintwork, usually heard when travelling at speed over rough ground. Excessive chain slap may be due to a chain that's too long.

Chain suck: When the chain sticks to the chainring and is pulled up into the gap between chainring and frame. If it gets wedged you'll stop suddenly and the frame may be damaged. Usually the result of worn or dirty transmission components.

Chain whip: Tool used to hold the cassette still while the *lock ring* is undone. If the cassette isn't held it'll just spin on the *freehub* when you attempt to undo the lock ring.

Chromoly: Generic term for a range of light, strong steel alloys that include chromium and molybdenum in their constituents.

Cleats: Shaped metal plates bolted to the underside of riding shoes that engage in *clipless* pedals.

Clutch mech: Rear derailleurs that include a mechanism to slow down the fore-aft movement of the cage to reduce *chain slap*. Called Shadow Plus by Shimano and Type Two by SRAM.

Coil spring: Wound spring made of steel or titanium, used in some suspension forks and rear shocks, especially those intended for extreme riding. Coil springs are reliable and robust, but have limited adjustability and are much heavier than *air springs*.

Compact drive: Early MTB transmissions used chainrings with between 24 and 48 teeth in various combinations. Compact transmissions use rings from 22 to 42 teeth, with an 11-tooth sprocket on the *cassette* to get the gear range back.

Compatibility: Before index shifting, there was a period in mountain bike history when everything worked with everything else to at least some degree. Today some parts are interchangeable between brands but not all – a SRAM 10-speed cassette will work fine in an otherwise Shimano-based transmission, but a SRAM rear shifter won't correctly operate a Shimano rear mech (or vice versa).

Cone spanners: Thin spanners used to access the adjustable cones on hubs with *cup and cone bearings*.

Cranks: The arms, usually aluminium, that transfer your pedalling efforts to the chainrings. The cranks are just the arms themselves – cranks with chainrings fitted are referred to as a chainset.

Crank-removing tool: Threaded tool used to pull cranks from *bottom bracket* axles. Only used on *square taper, Octalink, ISIS* and similar designs.

Crown race remover: Bladed tool used to drift the bottom *headset* race off the fork *steerer tube*.

Crown race setting tool: Tubular tool for fitting the bottom headset race to the fork *steerer tube*. The race needs to be a tight fit, hence the need for a tool.

Cup and cone bearings: Bearings that use loose balls and adjustable bearing surfaces. Still often found in hubs.

Damper: Oil-filled chamber containing a piston to slow down the movement of a suspension fork or shock. Rebound damping controls the speed at which the unit extends to full length; compression damping controls the speed at which it compresses over bumps.

Derailleur: A French invention, perfected by Shimano, which shifts the chain across the chainrings and sprockets. Also known as a mech.

Disc brakes: Brakes that use a small hub-mounted rotor rather than the wheel rim as a braking surface. Disc brakes are now standard fitment on mountain bikes, with only the very cheapest bikes using rim brakes.

Disc brake bleed kit: Collection of plastic tubes and syringes used to top up or replace the fluid in hydraulic brakes.

DOT 4 and 5: Two grades of brake fluid for hydraulic brakes. DOT 4 is based on ethylene glycol, DOT 5 is silicone-based. The two grades aren't interchangeable, so make sure you use the right one.

Drivetrain: Term for the whole transmission of the bike, from pedals to rear hub.

Elastomer: A special high-density plastic with elastic properties. Used to be common in suspension forks, but now mostly superseded by air springs.

Eyeletted rims: Reinforcing eyelets are used around the spoke holes in a rim to spread the nipple tension and build a stronger wheel.

Facing: Process of removing excess material from the frame to ensure correct alignment of components. Head tubes, bottom bracket shells and brake mounts should all be faced.

Ferrules: The metal or plastic caps used to finish the ends of gear and brake cable housing.

Flat bar: Handlebar with the ends at the same height as the centre, with just a gentle sweep between the two. Contrast with *riser bar*, which has the ends offset upwards relative to the centre.

Flange: The section of the wheel hub into which the spokes are hooked.

Flats: Pedals with a large, spiked platform used in combination with flat-soled shoes. Once the preserve of downhill riders and dirt jumpers, flats are increasingly popular for all-round riding too.

Forging: A manufacturing process for components and frame parts, essentially involving hammering a lump of metal into shape. The resulting part is very strong.

Frame: The central and main component of the bike, to which all the other parts are mounted.

Freehub mechanism: The part of a rear hub that only allows the sprockets to rotate in one direction, thus allowing you to coast without turning the pedals.

Full suspension: A bike with suspension units at front and rear. Compare *hardtail* and *rigid*.

Geometry: The lengths and angles of the frame tubes that govern how a bike reacts to rider inputs.

Granny gear: The smallest chainring, usually 22 teeth on a triple chainset. So called either because it's suitable for grannies to get up hills or simply because it doesn't have many teeth.

Grinder: Bench-mounted power tool used for smoothing the cut edges of metal parts. Also a colloquial term for a big crash.

Gripshift: Twist shifter made by SRAM. Very light and simple, although most riders prefer trigger shifters.

Gusset: Added reinforcement for frames, especially important around the head tube where extra sections are added to brace this highly-stressed area. Tube reinforcements are now often added by *hydroforming*.

Hardtail: A bike with a rigid frame and suspension fork.

Head angle: A steeper head angle has the effect of quickening and sharpening the steering. The trend is towards slacker head angles, giving more high-speed stability.

Headset: The bearings that allow the fork to turn in the frame to facilitate steering.

Headset cup remover: Rocket-shaped tool for hammering *headset* cups out of the frame.

Headset press: Threaded tool used to push *headset* cups into the frame.

Housing: The flexible outer casings that guide gear and brake cables along the frame. Gear housing is made using longitudinal steel strands so that it doesn't compress, allowing for accurate *indexing*.

Hubs: The rotating element at the centre of the wheel. May use either *cup and cone* or *cartridge* bearings. If *disc brakes* are used, the brake rotor will be mounted to the hub.

Hydroforming: Tube shaping process that uses high-pressure fluid to force the tube walls into a mould.

Allows complex shapes to be formed but requires thicker tube walls than traditional butted tubing.

Indexing: Gear system with shift levers that click once for each gear, making shifting easier.

Jockey wheels: Pair of small sprockets in the *rear mech* mounted in a sprung, pivoting cage that controls chain tension.

Machined rims: Rims are made from a strip of alloy, so have to be joined to form a circle. Machining the sidewalls of the rim ensures that there's no step at the join, giving smoother braking.

Ovalised tubing: Frame tubes that are formed with an oval cross-section instead of the traditional cylinder. A horizontal oval at the *bottom bracket* makes the frame stiffer under pedalling, while a vertical oval at the head tube means more weld area for strength.

PCD: Pitch Circle Diameter, the distance between the fixing bolts on chainrings.

Pivot point: where the suspension lever pivots. The further forward the pivot point, the plusher the suspension will be in the saddle (and firmer out of it). When the rider is seated there is greater leverage on the pivot point and hence the shock. As the rider stands the weight moves forward, thereby lessening the leverage and un-weighting the shock.

Plain gauge: Frame tubes that have the same wall thickness along their length, as opposed to *butted* tubes, which are thicker at the ends than in the centre. Can also refer to spokes.

Podger: See *bradawl*.

Quill stems: Handlebar stem that fits inside the fork steerer and is secured by an expanding wedge, rather than the later threadless headset system that uses a stem clamped to the outside of the steerer.

Rapidfire: Shimano's name for its twin-lever trigger shifters – press one lever to shift up, the other lever to shift down.

Rapid Rise: Also known as 'Low Normal', an ill-fated Shimano design that sprung the *rear derailleur* towards the large sprocket rather than the small one, reversing the action of the shifter.

Rear derailleur: See *rear mech*.

Rear shock: See *Shock*

Release agent: Tyre moulds are coated with a substance that prevents the rubber from sticking to the mould. This slippery coating can leave a residue on the tyres themselves, compromising grip until it's been scrubbed off from riding.

Remote lockout: Bar-mounted lever to lock the front or rear suspension to prevent it moving on smooth ground.

Replaceable hanger: The part of the frame to which the *rear derailleur* bolts is vulnerable to damage in a crash. On steel frames it can be bent back, but aluminium and carbon frames usually have bolt-on hangers that are easily replaced.

Rigid fork: Front fork with fixed legs, rather than a telescopic suspension fork. Unusual on new bikes but by no means extinct.

Rim brake: Brake that acts on the wheel rim to slow the bike.

Riser bars: Handlebars with a double bend to offset the grips upwards from the stem, giving a higher riding position.

Rocket tool: See *Headset cup remover*

Sag: the amount the suspension compresses as you simply sit on the bike.

Shock: Spring/damper unit used to suspend the back end of the bike.

Singletrack: A trail just wide enough for one bike. The most popular kind of trail to ride, especially if it has lots of corners.

Sliders: The lower legs of a suspension fork that move up and down on the stanchions.

Snakebite: Also known as 'pinch flats'. A puncture caused by hitting an object on the trail hard enough to squash the tyre flat against the rim, pinching the inner tube and forming a distinctive double hole.

SPD: Shimano Pedalling Dynamics, the name of the most common type of *clipless* pedal system that holds your feet to the pedals using cleats attached to the shoes. A spring-loaded mechanism means you can disengage from the pedals simply by twisting your foot outwards.

Spider: The part of the crank that attaches the chainrings to the cranks.

Spoke tension meter: Device for measuring how tight the spokes of a wheel are. Spoke tensions need to be even for a long-lasting wheel.

Sprockets: The toothed wheels at the back of the bike with which the chain engages to drive the rear wheel.

Stanchion: The fixed legs of a suspension fork, along which the lower legs slide up and down.

Star-fangled nut: Spiked nut that fits into the top of the fork and has the headset top cap threaded into it.

Tightening the top cap increases the preload on the *headset* bearings to eliminate play.

Stiction: Contraction of static friction, the resistance to initial movement of a suspension fork or shock due to seal drag.

Suspension-corrected geometry: Frame geometry designed for use with suspension forks, which are typically longer than rigid forks. Most hardtail frames are now suitable for forks with 100–120mm of travel. Older frames from the 1990s may only handle well with 80mm or even less travel.

Thumb shifter: The first style of gear shift for mountain bikes, with a single bar-mounted lever to pull the gear cable. Originally used friction or a ratchet to stay in position and relied on the rider to move the lever just the right amount to change gear. Later models were indexed, making shifting easier.

Toeclips and straps: Method for keeping your feet on the pedals, very popular before *clipless* pedals came along. Toestraps are still useful for holding bikes to roofracks, attaching spare inner tubes under saddles and so on.

Top-out: A knocking caused by the suspension rebounding too quickly due to insufficient damping or too high a spring rate. Some budget suspension forks top out however they're adjusted. Using all the suspension travel is known as 'bottoming out'.

Tubeless tyres: Tyres with a special locking bead designed to work without inner tubes, making pinch punctures less likely and allowing lower tyre pressures for better grip.

Warehouse bike: See *BSO*.

INDEX